Dash o Doric:
THE HALE LOT

Dash o Doric:

THE HALE LOT

Robbie Shepherd
and
Norman Harper

Birlinn

This edition first published in Great Britain in 2003
by Birlinn Ltd
West Newington House
10 Newington Road
Edinburgh EH9 1QS

www.birlinn.co.uk

A catalogue record is available on request
from the British Library

ISBN 1 84158 250 6

Typeset by Palimpsest Book Production Limited,
Polmont, Stirlingshire
Printed and bound by Cox & Wyman, Reading

Contents

Foreword

ONE of the features of a newspaper columnist's life, as Robbie and I know, is the morning mailbag. Sometimes it's light. Sometimes it's heavy. Always, it's a useful barometer of what interests the readership and what does not.

From time to time, when I used to write a Wednesday column for the *Press and Journal*, I would chance my arm and stray from the strict English-language brief and venture into the realms of the Doric. Always, without exception, those columns drew the highest number of responses from readers throughout northern Scotland.

Indeed, the biggest mailbag I received in nearly twenty-seven years on the newspaper was after a column which I confess I had put together in something of a hurry (a deadline is marvellous inspiration). In it, I outlined the five Doric words that, to me, were most evocative. They were the words that conjured the most vivid pictures and sounded lush and meaty.

As I recall, the five were contermacious, blaad, swick, tyauve and dubs. If you've bought this book as a self-respecting Doric speaker, you shouldn't need me to translate, so I won't. I finished by inviting readers to jot down their own favourites if they had time and send them. *If* they had time.

I had expected perhaps a couple of dozen letters, but for the whole of the following week the mail poured in by sack, fax, voicemail and e-mail. There could still be a couple of carrier pigeons up on the Lang Stracht roof, for all I know.

There was so much mail listing favourite Doric words that I had to stop counting after several hundreds. I certainly hadn't a hope of replying to any. I was pleased, of course, that the readers had responded so well. I was intrigued to see that one particular word topped the poll by a long, long margin. More than anything, I was delighted that my long-held conviction that the Doric was far from dead had been proved so emphatically.

People revel in its use. They respond enthusiastically when given the opportunity, be that via newspaper columns, church services or evening classes. All the Doric needs is a channel. In these days when the Scottish Executive appears to consider that Urdu and Cantonese deserve more official attention and respect than it can provide for one of the country's native tongues, I fear there is little hope of that. For the moment, then, in the absence of any worthwhile support from those who should be ashamed of themselves for the lack, we have to be content to provide our own amusement.

This anthology combines the first two Dash o Doric books as a precursor to a third, all-new volume which the two of us will be delivering shortly. We hope you enjoy the tales. As far as we can tell, all are genuine. Those which we had heard before or which had a familiar fictional ring to them, but which were too good to abandon altogether, we grouped in the back of the book on their own. Take them with a pinch of salt.

And, by the way, the north of Scotland's favourite Doric word is ... (drum roll, open gold envelope) ... forfochen.

Enjoy your book.

Norman Harper and Robbie Shepherd
October, 2003

PUBLISHER'S NOTE

This omnibus edition combines the text of *Dash o Doric* and *Anither Dash o Doric*.

Each chapter in this edition starts with the text from *Dash o Doric* and ends with the material from the corresponding chapter in *Anither Dash o Doric*.

Babes and Sucklings

Some of the best humour from any part of the world spills from the mouths of children. That's as true of the North-east as anywhere, as this selection proves.

A MRS Yule wrote from Ellon to tell us of a neighbour, a young mum, who visited one day with her unruly son. The boy was clearly in no mood for discipline and scraped ornaments across the sideboard and threw cushions on to the floor.

'I didn't like to say anything,' wrote Mrs Yule. 'But when the boy started kicking the furniture, I coughed and glared at him. The young mother finally decided to act. "Lee!" she shouted. "Stop kickin the furniture. Ye'll spile yer new sheen."'

A THREE-YEAR-OLD from Gamrie was being corrected in his speech by his future aunt. All the best people from Gamrie are very broadly spoken, and he was certainly one of the best. At one point, he began a lively discourse on his 'moo'.

His aunt-to-be remonstrated. 'Andrew, that's your mouth, not your moo.'

He considered this for a moment. His aunt pointed to either side of his head. 'And these are your ears.'

Some time after, his grannie noticed him feeling around his head and asked if he had a problem.

'OK, Grunnie,' he said, feeling his ears, 'if this is ma ears, far's ma lugs?'

A YOUNG father on his two weeks onshore from the rigs was picking up his five-year-old son, who had just started school at a primary not a million miles from Turriff.

'And fit did ye learn the day?' inquired Dad.

The boy fixed him with a stare.

'That ither loons get pocket money.'

A PORTSOY mother was concerned that her eight-year-old, David, had picked up some rather fruity language. As mothers do, she blamed his playmates, and the other mothers blamed David. His mother was still concerned and asked the town bobby to have a word with her son to see if that might scare it out of him.

One day, as David was wandering home alone from school, the bobby spotted him, crossed the street slowly and stopped in front of him.

'Well, David,' he said in the sternest tone he could muster. 'I hear ye've been usin bad language.'

'Fa telt ye that?' said David.

'Oh,' said the bobby, 'a wee bird happened ontil ma windae-sill and he telt me a aboot it.'

'The dirty bugger,' said David. 'And efter me feedin them ivry mornin.'

IN THE days of thatched cottages, one of the foremost thatchers was Adam Clyne. One morning at school, the children of one thackit hoosie were among a class being taught the Bible.

'Now,' said the teacher, Miss McIntosh, 'does anyone know about Adam?'

'Aye,' said one child. 'He's thackin wir hoose aenoo.'

RETIRED BANKER Edwin Reid tells of a six-year-old who was asked what he wanted for his birthday and who replied: 'An Autobank card.'

'An Autobank card? Fit wye?'

'Because ye get siller fanivver ye wint.'

A CHILD was asked by his primary teacher why his sister was absent from school.

'Please, miss,' said the wee lad, 'she's got a blin lump on her doup and she canna sit doon.'

'Her what?' said the teacher.

The pupil couldn't think for a wee while, then suggested: 'Please, miss, her dock.'

'Try again,' said the exasperated teacher.

The lad replied: 'Her aarse.'

In the end, admitting defeat but pointing out the error in his language, she snapped: 'Oh, sit down on your bottom,' which brought snickering around the class.

At playtime, naturally, the discussion centred on the exchange in the classroom. This brought a pensive murmur from the wee lad, who said: 'Weel, she *his* a blin lump on her erse.'

A FIRST-YEAR pupil at Fraserburgh Academy arrived late one morning for a first-period science class. When asked by the teacher for an explanation for his tardiness, he replied quite naturally: 'Sorry, miss, bit ma mither wis darnin a hole in the erse o ma brikks.'

No sooner were the words uttered than he flushed, clapped his hands to his mouth and stuttered apologetically: 'Oh, I'm sorry, miss. I mean ma troosers.'

DURING THE war, many city people sought the relative safety of the countryside and, with a post as teacher at a nearby village, Mrs Raey rented a cottar hoose from one farming family. Young Jimmy, a boisterous four-year-old and son of the grieve at Cluny Home Farm, soon made himself acquant with daily visits, and often when the lady was in the middle of baking.

One day, he asked for a drink of milk. Mrs Raey filled the cup and handed it to the little boy, saying: 'Take care now, Jimmy; the cup is full.'

Jimmy proceeded to examine the cup, turning it round and round in his wee hands and said finally in a puzzled tone: 'It's nae fool ata, Mrs Raey. It's clean.'

ONE ASSISTANT editor with the *Press and Journal* tells

of games he used to play when his two sons were small and they would try to guess what would be for tea on any given night. If their guess was wrong, he would tell them: 'Wrang spy.'

The game became a regular feature in advance of meal-times until one day when the second boy was old enough to be asked what he would like for his tea. He thought for a few moments, then said firmly: 'I'd like some o that Rang's Pie.'

ONE OF your co-authors has a younger brother who is still mightily embarrassed to be reminded of the day, when he was four or five, that the tyres on his tricycle went flat while he was visiting his grandfather, and he became very perplexed.

'Fit'll we dee, Ian?' asked his grandfather. 'Ye've nae air in yer tyres.'

Ian thought for a few moments, then his little face brightened. 'I ken, granda,' he said. 'We'll tak the air oot o Norman's tyres.'

IT WAS the boy's first day at a rural school and, coming home in a foul mood, he was faced by his mother who was asking how he had got on.

'I'm nae gyaun back,' he replied firmly. 'I canna read. I canna write. And the wifie winna let me spik.'

THIS ONE is a famous North-east story and came to us in several different forms, so we have no doubt that it is true. The most common variation on the theme depicted a mother and a restless son of about four on a bus heading from Aberdeen out to Ellon. Across the gangway from them was another, younger mother and her new baby. It was obviously feeding time – judging by the continuous crying of the little one – which attracted the attention of the fidgety four-year-old.

As nature decreed, the young mum started breast-feeding the baby. The four-year-old stared in disbelief.

His mother pulled his shoulder. 'Feeding time,' she whispered. 'Now stop starin.'

'Bit mam!' he said, his eyes growing ever wider, 'he canna aet a that athoot a tattie.'

AN ALFORD minister's wife in the 1960s used to tell of being invited to judge a children's cookery contest in the village hall and, unusually for those days, spotted a small boy as one of the contestants. He had made iced queen cakes, and when she stood in front of him she made a great show of tasting the queen cakes and saying how delicious they were. He glowed with pride.

'And tell me,' she said. 'You have such a lovely gloss on your icing. How do you manage that?'

'I lick them.'

A CONJUROR was enthralling his young audience at a Supporters' Club Children's Christmas Party at Huntly in the early 1970s. One of his tricks involved pulling eggs from a hat. As he pulled the umpteenth egg from the depths of his topper, he turned to one wee lad at the end of the front row and called: 'I bet your mother can't get eggs without hens.'

'Aye, she can,' replied the boy. 'She keeps dyeucks.'

A GAMEKEEPER at Duff House, Banff, at the turn of the century was telling his wife one night of the arrangements for the Duke of Fife's return from the Continent, and that the Duke would drive round by his lodge.

Next morning, the gamie's daugher, aged three, looked up into her mother's face and asked: 'I say, mam, will we open the gate for the dyeuck, or will he jist flee ower?'

BILL WILSON, of Peterhead, reports being on holiday

in Majorca and staying at the same hotel as a young couple with two children, obviously from somewhere in the North-east.

One sunny morning, the boy, aged about six, ran to his mother. 'Mam, can I dive in the sweemin-pool?'

'No, it's ower deep for ye.'

'Bit Dad's in.'

'He's insured.'

DUNCAN FORBES, now of Elgin, tells a story from almost 30 years ago, when his five-year-old, Selina, was very quiet when she was supposed to be out the back of the house playing. Duncan fancied it was just a little too quiet and was about to go out to investigate when Selina came in through the back door.

'Fit hiv ye been deein, Selina?' asked her dad.

'Cleanin the dog's teeth,' said Selina.

'I hope ye hinna hurtit the doggie.'

'No, dad,' said Selina. 'And I'll pit back yer toothbrush, jist like I aye dee.'

A YOUNG Ellon mother was horrified when her five-year-old returned from school with his clothes torn and dirty and his face, arms and legs covered in bruises. The other boys had been throwing stones at him on the way home, he admitted.

'Well,' said his mother, 'we'd better sort this oot. Fit's their names?'

'I dinna ken their names.'

'Well, ye'd better tell yer teacher the morn. We canna pit up wi this. Bullyin needs nippin in the bud.'

'I dinna like tellin the teacher.'

'Well, if it happens again, dinna you start throwing steens back at them. You come and get me.'

'Bit you're nae eese at throwin steens.'

ONE OF your co-authors still gets mightily embarrassed

when a hardy annual tale does the rounds of his family. It concerns his first school football match, when he arrived home tired, sore and dirty, but with a glow of immense satisfaction.

'And foo did ye get on?' asked his mother.

'Jist great,' he said, his little chest puffing out with pride. 'I scored a foul.'

... and from *Anither Dash o Doric*

THE LATE Betty Watson, of Ordhead, Cluny, was a Sunday School teacher in the district and was telling her class the story of how Pharaoh's daughter found the baby Moses floating in a basket among the bullrushes.

A young laddie's voice piped up: 'Aye, that wis her story.'

AT THE same Sunday School at Cluny, to see if they had been paying attention, Miss Watson started asking questions and when asking what an epistle was was given the answer:

'Is't apostle's wife?'

YVONNE CORMACK lived at Aboyne in the mid-1970s and recalls an evening of one of the fiercest thunder-and-lightning storms she had experienced. She was nervous enough for herself, but she was concerned that her six-year-old, Christopher, tucked safely upstairs in bed, would be beside himself with terror.

Yvonne made her way upstairs and, flinching between cracks of thunder and flashes of lightning, listened outside Christopher's room. She could hear a small voice from inside the bedroom, but couldn't make out what he was saying.

As quietly as she could, she opened the door to find Christopher standing on top of the small toy chest in front of the bedroom window, curtains opened, eyes wide with excitement and clapping his hands and squealing with delight:

'Bang it again, God. Bang it again.'

LATER, WHEN Christopher was a year older, and Yvonne became pregnant with her second child, she sat Christopher down and explained what was happening. With a very serious look on his face, he considered all the implications.

Then Yvonne added: 'So I doot we'll hae ti move hoose, Christopher.'

Christopher looked up: 'Will the baby nae folly us and find oot far we are?'

AS A CHILD, Margaret Mathison, of Edinburgh, spent her summer holidays in a Banffshire fishing town, where one of her playmates lived with her granny. Granny had brought up the entire family, but always welcomed Margaret into her home for a chat.

The oldest grand-daughter had moved South to go into service and, in due course, had wed and had given birth to a son.

Margaret happened to visit on the day the baby arrived at great-grandma's home for the first time.

'Did ye ken that oor Jeannie's gotten a loonie?' enquired the new great-grandma.

'Oh, that's good news,' said Margaret.

'And div ye ken fit she's ca'ed him?' said great-grandma. 'No.'

'She's ca'ed him Keith.'

'Oh,' said Margaret.

'Gweed sakes,' said great-grandma with a dry snort of disapproval, 'she micht as weel hiv ca'ed him Fochabers.'

A KEITH teacher was told by one of her infant class that he had a new baby brother. 'Oh, how super,' she said, 'and what's he called?'

'Spot.'

'Spot? That's a strange name. Are you sure?'

'Spot,' repeated the boy firmly.

It wasn't until a few days later, when she met the new-born's mother in town, that the mystery was cleared up.

The baby's name was Mark.

JESS ROBERTSON, now of Dundee, recalls her son, David, going back to Oldmeldrum Primary School after the summer holidays and stepping up from Primary Two to Primary Three.

When he returned home after his first day, Jess asked him how things had been and if he had liked his new teacher.

'She wis the same as the last een,' he said. 'Jist a different heid.'

MELISSA WAS fascinated with the news that the young couple next door had had a baby boy, and phoned her grandma at Inverurie to tell her the news.

'That's good news, Melissa,' said Grandma. 'And fit are they ca'in him?'

Melissa hesitated for a moment, then said: 'Chewed. They're ca'in him Chewed.'

'Chewed?'

'Chewed.'

Only later did Grandma discover that the problem had arisen because Melissa's mum insisted on the Queen's English at all times and didn't want her drifting into the Doric.

The baby's name was Chad.

DAVID RETURNED home from his first day back at school at Mintlaw Primary and his mother was anxious to know how he had got on.

'Fit did ye learn, David?'

'Nithing.'

'Ye must hiv learned something.'

'Well, the wifie wintit ti ken foo ti spell HORSE, so I jist telt her and she didna bother me efter 'at.'

YOUNG MICHAEL was definitely his father's son. Only five, he strode about the farm with his wee chestie puffed out, thumbs in the straps of his specially made dungars, eyeing up the nowt and sitting with the farm labourers at fly time.

Eventually there came an addition to the family, a baby sister, and Michael's aunt from Aberdeen asked him if he was pleased with the new baby.

'Fairly that,' he said, scowling as he hauled off his wee wellies. 'Though we'd mair need o a new ploo.'

KENNETHMONT HALL was the scene of a fiddlers' recital one evening in the early 1970s. A fair number of children had been brought along, for these were the days before childminders and babysitters.

Evidently, fiddle music wasn't quite the cup of tea of one young man, for during the first fiddle solo, his voice floated across the crowd:

'Mam, dis he stop fin he cuts his box in twa?'

WE TAKE you to a geography lesson in a school where it was frowned upon to use the mither tongue. Only standard English was acceptable.

Doris Bruce, of Montrose, taught in Muirfield Primary School in Aberdeen some thirty-five years ago. She discovered that her Primary Five pupils knew nothing about the Channel Isles, so she decided on a little lesson there and then.

A few days later, Miss Bruce asked: 'Now, who can remember the names of some of those islands?'

Well, she got Jersey and Guernsey and then they stuck.

At last, a lass who never said much put up her hand. 'Please, miss,' she started. 'Sh-sh-sh-sh', and then she halted with a sudden look of horror.

'Yes, Elizabeth?'

'Shirt.'

ALL THE way from Victoria, Australia, came this reminder of early school days back home, from Norah Hardy.

At the beginning of one term, a poor wee chap turned up all on his own for his very first day at school. Of course, he had to be registered.

'What's your name?'

'Jimmy Gordon.'

'What's your father's name?'

'I dinna ken.'

'Well, what does your mother call him?'

'A coorse bugger.'

THE PUPILS at Rayne North School were asked if they knew any poems by Robert Burns. Elsie stood up and started to recite:

'Wee sleekit, coorin, timrous beastie

'Oh, what a bannock's in thy breastie.'

ETHEL BAIRD, of Kincorth, tells of visiting a neighbour to see the new baby and finding four-year-old Robert sitting on the sofa in the front room with a face like thunder.

'Are ye prood o yer new baby brither, Robert?' she enquired.

But Robert said nothing.

'Fa div ye think he's like?'

Still nothing.

'I wid say he's got yer dad's nose and yer mither's een.'

'Aye,' said Robert, 'and he's got my bedroom.'

Sweet Bird of Doric Wit

The future of any sense of humour lies in its teenagers and young adults. We're happy to report that the Doric sense of humour appears to be hale and hearty – although often unwittingly.

A PETERHEAD joiner had taken on an apprentice who was full of boundless enthusiasm, but who didn't appear to have a great deal of commonsense.

'Foo d'ye ken if ye should use a nail or a screw?' asked the joiner one morning, by way of a test.

The apprentice thought for a minute. 'Use a nail first,' he said. 'And then?' said the joiner.

'And then if the wid splits, use a screw.'

A TURRIFF lad who had had immense difficulty in finding regular work after leaving school had been signed up to the Shore Porters in Aberdeen, one of the world's oldest, most celebrated and most trusted furniture-removal firms.

When, a few weeks later, a neighbour asked his mother how Norman was getting on, she said: 'Oh, fine, fine. He's jist hid the one mischanter. He broke an expinsive Chinese pot at a hoose in Hamilton Place, and they say it wis worth near three hunder poun. So they've telt him they'll be takkin the cost oot o his wages at three poun a wikk.'

'What rare,' said the neighbour. 'A steady job at last.'

A CLERK at a Banff law practice had struggled to make ends meet on his meagre income and finally, urged by his parents to do something about it, sought an audience with the senior partner to see if a rise wasn't in order.

The senior partner listened to the tale, but declined to offer any more money, saying that times were difficult, and so on.

As the dejected lad turned to go, the partner said: 'I

can see you're disappointed, and I suppose you've often wondered what you would do if you had my salary, eh?'

'No,' said the lad, closing the door, 'bit I've often winnered fit ee wid dee if ee hid mine.'

AN ABERDEEN florist was waxing proud about his two children, one of whom had been accepted for Glasgow University to study medicine.

'Aye,' he said, puffing out his chest. 'I suppose ye could say – me bein a florist – that I've produced a buddin genius.'

'Aye,' muttered one nearby man to another. 'A peety the ither een's a bloomin eediot.'

ONE SMART young chap from Banchory was a student on a business-studies course at the old Robert Gordon's Institute of Technology in Aberdeen, and had been asked by the lecturer which magnate he would nominate as the world's most successful businessman.

The Deesider thought for a few moments, then said: 'Noah.'

The lecturer and all of the class were surprised, to say the least, and the lecturer demanded to know how the student had come to that conclusion.

'Well,' grinned the student. 'Noah managed to float a limited company at a time when the rest of the world was going into liquidation.'

A MR ELLIS, from Ballater, wrote to tell us of the summer he was out walking in the Deeside woods when he came upon a group of seven or eight primary-school boys flinging sticks and stones up a tree. As he drew closer, he realised their target was a red squirrel, now beside itself with fright.

'Hie!' he shouted. 'What do you think you're doing?'

The boys spun round, saw him and were decently embarrassed. It took the ringleader to explain: 'It's OK mister, we wis only tryin ti knock it doon so we could stroke it.'

ONE RECRUITING sergeant at the Aberdeen Army Careers Office tells the story of the raw North-east country lad who turned up determined to be a soldier. Despite his scrawniness and a suspicious look of being under-age, the sergeant was impressed with the lad's determination.

'How fit are you?' he boomed.

'Five fit, three inch.'

NOW THAT it is more common to see young dads pushing prams in the park, Ethel Baird, of Kincorth, tells us of seeing a young father pushing a pram round the Duthie Park in Aberdeen and mumbling something gently towards the occupant.

As he came closer to the park bench where she was feeding pigeons, she heard that he was saying: 'That's it, Darren, ye're deein fine. Jist relax. Ye're deein gran. Nae bother, Darren. It'll be OK.'

She smiled and, as they passed, congratulated him on keeping up a dialogue with his son. 'You fairly know how to speak to a baby,' she said. 'Quietly and gently.'

She stood up, leaned over the pram and said: 'And what seems to be the matter with Darren, anyway?'

'No,' said the young dad. 'He's Alan. I'm Darren.'

AN OLD farmer who didn't believe in bad weather set the men to work one absolutely foul day.

'A them that his ileskins can gyang oot and pu neeps,' he barked.

'And fit aboot us that disna hae ileskins?' said one young lad.

'Aye,' said the farmer, 'you can dee likewise.'

THE SAME farmer was dead against smoking, and when he caught the orraloon lighting up a Woodbine up the farm close, he stopped:

'Ye can tak that thing oot o yer face, min, and keep yer win for yer wark.'

NANCY FORSYTH wrote to tell us of her brother, Frankie, starting his apprenticeship in a garage. One day, an extremely elegant and self-important woman couldn't get her car into the garage because a lorry was parked across the entrance. She asked the lorry-driver to move the lorry, but he replied that he couldn't for a few minutes and that she would have to wait.

The woman was indignant. She puffed herself out to her full girth and snapped: 'Do you know who I am?'

The driver leaned round the side of the lorry and called to the new apprentice: 'Frunkie, awa and phone the doctor. This wifie disna ken fa she is.'

A YOUTH was lounging at a country crossroads when a man in a Riley Pathfinder stopped and asked for directions to Kinnoir. The youth never took his hands out of his pockets, but jerked his elbow in the direction of Kinnoir.

The Riley man was taken aback at the youth's slovenliness and said: 'You know, if anyone can show me a lazier trick than that, I'd be bound to give them a fiver.'

The youth, still with his hands in his pockets, stretched the pockets enough to show a space between his hands and the material and said: 'Pit it there.'

NORMAN MELDRUM, from Banff, was a champion schools debater, representing Banff Academy several times in the *Press and Journal* schools debating competition in the mid-1980s.

In 1987, he was part of the year's runner-up team, for whom the prize was a weekend's all-expenses-paid trip to London. Part of the trip involved visiting the Greenwood Theatre for the Thursday-night taping of *Question Time*, the BBC TV discussion programme chaired then by Sir Robin Day.

Out of an audience of 300 people, it was Norman who was chosen to put the first question of the evening, on national television, to a panel of four of the country's most senior politicians, including David Owen and Joan Lestor. It was quite a task for a 16-year-old, but he carried it off with customary aplomb.

After the taping, the *Press and Journal* guests were invited into the post-recording canapés-and-wine party, attended by the production team, the political guests, a couple of Government ministers and one or two other VIPs. When Sir Robin was told that there were champion schools debaters in the assembly, he made a point of crossing the reception room to talk to them, and remembered at once that it was Norman whose question had opened the show. He congratulated him for the way he had phrased it.

'But tell me,' he said, 'I hope you weren't nervous at posing such a tough question to four of the country's most exalted notables – and on national television, too.'

'Na, na,' said Norman. 'I've been on the stage wi Robbie Shepherd.'

ONE DEESIDE builder was growing more and more frustrated with his teenage son and the lad's seeming reluctance to fix on any career. Eventually, the father decided to start him off on an apprenticeship in the building firm.

When a builder from a nearby village called in one day looking for some spare supplies, he spotted the young lad slouched in a corner of the yard, looking glumly at some two by four.

'How's the loon gettin on?' he asked.

'He's a miracle-worker,' said the father.

The visitor brightened. 'Is that so?' he said. 'Well, I'm richt pleased ti hear it, for I kent ye werena affa sure aboot the deal ata.'

'No, he's a miracle-worker, richt enough,' said the father again. 'If ivver he dis ony work, it's a bliddy miracle.'

. . . and from *Anither Dash o Doric*

A LETTER from Donald McAllister, of Banff, reported that his son, Derek, now a happily married man with a grown-up family, was a beatnik (or as close as Banff could manage) in the 1960s, with all the paraphernalia of Beatlemania – the shaggy haircut, tight trousers, steel comb and Mini Traveller passionwagon.

He and his friends had decided to go for a week's holiday to London, presumably to enhance their wardrobes in Carnaby Street and to do the rounds of the clubs.

After a few tinctures one evening, they had tumbled out of a club, high on John Barleycorn, and had fallen straight at the feet of a London bobby.

The bobby watched as they picked themselves up and calmed themselves down then, studying their winklepickers, asked with a mild hint of a sneer: 'Do your feet really fit those shoes?'

'Aye,' said Derek. 'Dis your heid really fit that hat?'

HOME FROM Edinburgh University, Donna Hendry, of Banchory, noticed that her grandmother, who lived with the family, had taken a sudden notion for reading the Bible, and every spare minute was spent with her nose in the good book.

Donna's mother had also noticed and, she tells us, mentioned the fact to Donna.

'Dinna worry aboot it,' said Donna reassuringly. 'She's jist studyin for her finals.'

DURING THE war, when many a raw young North-east loon found himself in the deserts of North Africa, a sergeant with the background of Perwinnes rather than the Pyrenees was drilling his men near the pyramids of Egypt and was frustrated to find that the young squaddies' eyes kept wandering towards the monuments.

Eventually, the sergeant lost his rag.

'Fit the hell are ye glowerin at?' he bawled. 'A rickle o aul steens. His neen o ye seen Bennachie?'

NEGLECT THE perspective of the bairns of the North-east at your peril. They're taking in everything to store for future use when the occasion arises.

Jimmy Glennie, of Inverurie, told of the lad watching the morning ritual in the bathroom before the day's work had really begun. He enquired: 'Dad, fit wye's yer hair makkin that cracklin soon?'

'That's the electric comin aff fin I comb it.'

A wee while later, he spotted his mother.

'Mam, fit wye's yir belly makkin at queer soon?'

'Must be something I've aeten. Jist a bittie gas.'

Next day, the lad was playing outside with his pal whose parents were doing rather well from the work in the oil industry and the five-year-old son of the rigger wasn't slow in coming forward to say so.

'My dad's got plenty money. They're jist back fae a holiday in Hong Kong.'

There was a moment's hesitation and a moment's jealousy until our young hero brightened:

'That's nithing; my dad's got electric in his heid and ma mam's got gas in her belly.'

AN INFORMED source – a retired Garioch teacher who sought anonymity – recalled overhearing two young lads who were discussing the forthcoming school play in which one of them had to kiss the heroine.

'I've nivver tried es kissin afore,' confided one to the other. 'Fit wye div ye dee't?'

'It's easy,' said one. 'Jist steek yer moo lik ye wis sookin a pandrop.'

CHARLES BARRON, Arts Director of the Haddo Arts Trust, told us of his days as a young teacher at Inverurie

Academy and being landed last thing on a Friday with a difficult class 1S.

They were not the most academically gifted, and one Friday, as in the previous three or four weeks, he had been hammering home gender equivalents. For example, the female form of master is mistress; the female form of ram is ewe, and so on.

Sandy was a richt fine loon, but always the slowest of the class at answering.

However, this Friday, Charles came to the female equivalent of duke and, to his astonishment, Sandy's hand went up.

Face flushed with excitement, hair standing on end with effort, Sandy delivered his answer with all the confidence of the man who knows, beyond all question, that he is right.

'Drake,' he said. 'A wifie deuk's a drake.'

IT MIGHT have been three of the same lads who were asked in another Inverurie Academy class to name the odd man out among potato, cabbage and knife.

'Knife,' said the first. 'The ither twa's veggies.'

'Knife,' said the second. 'It's the only een wi metal in't.'

'Cubbidge,' said the third.

'Cabbage?' said the teacher. 'How do you work that out?'

'Ye can mak chips wi the ither twa.'

DURING A school inspection at an Aberdeenshire academy in the early 1960s, the inspector sat down beside a 14-year-old and began discussing his work and looking at the books in his desk.

Eventually, during a lull in proceedings, the boy got up and asked his teacher who the man was. She explained that he was a schools inspector and that the boy should answer whatever questions were put to him.

He went back to his desk, sat for a while, then asked for permission to go out to the basket to sharpen his pencil. After a while, his teacher said: 'Now, you've been sharpening that pencil long enough. You can go back to your desk.'

'I canna,' he whispered.

'Why not?'

'Yon detective's still at it. He's surely lookin for clues.'

WHILE WORKING for the co-opie butcher in his youth, Donald Manson was put to making sausages. He declares himself appalled at what went into them and, worse still, at one point he stumbled while carrying sawdust and some of the sawdust went into the mixture waiting to go into the skins.

'I went, trembling, to the boss,' wrote Donald. 'I said: "I've drappit saadust in the sassidges, I'm soarry." '

'Na, na,' soothed the boss. 'There's nithing lik an improved recipe.'

JAMES MORRISON, now of Urybank, recalls his days as a fee'd loon and attending the dances in the old distillery at Jericho, near Colpy. The band was put at one end of a loft so long that the music could barely be heard at the other end.

The loft was reached by a set of stone stairs outside – without railings, of course.

Charlie Nicol and Doug Allardyce were two fairm loons who liked a dram. One dance night, they had a fair whack o the barley-bree and, when they decided to go home, Charlie led the way.

But Charlie forgot about the stair and stepped over the side, fell off the top and landed on his back in a bed of nettles.

He was so anaesthetised that he was not badly hurt – just stung all over – but, anxious that his pal didn't meet the same fate, he raised his head and shouted:

'Doug! Watch that first step! She's a bugger!'

Kissies and Bosies

The North-east's romantic attachments are no different from anywhere else's, except that we don't talk about them as much. Perhaps these few examples will explain why.

MRS JEAN Macfarlane was a census-taker at Peterhead in 1971 before moving to Edinburgh. She recalls visiting one home in the town where a trachled-looking woman with six children aged between about two months and seven years came to the door. She was invited in and installed herself on the living-room settee.

In the course of the interview, the woman explained that her husband had died four years previously.

Mrs Macfarlane looked at the brood and wondered.

'I'm sorry,' she said. 'Maybe I misunderstood you. Did you say your husband died four years ago?'

'Aye,' said the woman then, catching the drift, added: 'He deed. I didna.'

A FRASERBURGH woman of somewhat slack reputation between the wars became the object of great interest in the community after she claimed she had been raped in the dark by a council roadman while walking home from a dance at Strichen.

'I dinna believe a word o't,' said one bustling matron to another as they queued for their groceries. 'I mean, foo did she ken it wis a roader if it wis in the dark?' 'Weel,' said the other. 'She'd likely hid ti dee a the work.'

A NEW Pitsligo man had been discovered in flagrante with a rather attractive widow from a nearby parish. Small villages being small villages, his wife got to hear about it and confronted him as he arrived home from work.

'There's nithing atween's,' he protested.

'Aye,' she said. 'Nae even a bliddy nichtgoon.'

A WOMAN wearing a large flowery hat arrived at a wedding at Portgordon Church in 1962 and was met by a very young and nervous usher who stopped her and asked: 'Are you a frien o the groom?'

'No,' said the woman. 'I'm the bride's mother.'

JOHN AND Jean from Buckie had been courting for a long number of years – thirty, to be exact – but there had never been a word of marriage until one day John said shyly:

'Jean, is it nae aboot time we wis thinkin o gettin mairriet?'

'Behave yersel, John,' said Jean. 'Fa wid hae ony o us noo?'

JIMMY HAD taken a fancy to a young lass from near Alford, but couldn't quite work out how to ask for her hand in marriage, for these were the days when fathers could still make or break a courtship.

Meg's father had a forbidding bluntness and brusqueness about him, like many farmers of his vintage, and he wasn't about to give his daughter's hand to just anyone, least of all anyone who couldn't stand up to him.

As a result, Jimmy had been slow to pluck up the courage. Little did he know it, but he had an ally in Meg's mother, who had a soft spot for him and thought that her husband had been bordering on the cruel towards the young suitor.

'I widna be surprised supposin Jimmy his a question ti ask ye, Wullie,' said Meg's mother idly one day, beginning the softening-up process.

'Oh, aye, and fit wid that be?'

'I think he's maybe hearin waddin bells.'

'Is he noo? Waddin bells? We'll see aboot that.'

'Now, Wullie. You behave yersel. And fin the time comes and he asks yer blessin, dinna you be coorse til the loon. Be nice til him.'

A few Sundays later, Jimmy turned up at an uncommon

early hour before church. Meg and her mother were in the scullery.

'Is he in?' said Jimmy wanly.

'Oot the back shavin afore the Kirk,' said Meg's mother, urging him through.

Jimmy took a deep breath and shambled through to where Wullie was stooping over a basin.

'Aye-aye,' said Jimmy, by way of introduction.

Wullie looked round, then carried on shaving.

'Fine day,' said Jimmy.

'Mmphmm.'

There was an awkward pause. 'I've something ti speir at ye.'

'Oh aye.'

'A question, like.'

'Speir awa.'

'Well, I wis winderin if we could get mairriet.'

Wullie wiped the last of the soap from his face and turned to face Jimmy square on. 'Fa?' he said. 'You and me?'

A DONSIDE farmer's wife had been putting on a little more weight than was healthy and had amassed a formidable array of double chins. Still aware that her looks should be important to her, she sought a little reassurance from her husband that he still found her attractive.

'Div ye think I'm affa fat, Jock?' she inquired tentatively.

'Not a bit, quine,' he assured her.

'Is that richt, Jock?' she asked, secretly delighted.

'Richt enough,' he said, turning back to his paper. 'Mind you, there's whiles I think ye're keekin at me ower a pile o bannocks.'

NORTH-EAST man (and woman) are not known for being very demonstrative with their public affections, but one woman was a little more forthcoming with her marital *dis*affections. Overheard at a Garioch flower show in the late 1980s, she told her companion in a stage whisper: 'Aye, the only thing ma man and me's got in common is an anniversary on the same day.'

AN OLD couple decided they would try to recapture the vigour of their courtship and romance by booking into their honeymoon hotel for the night, decades after the event.

At bedtime, Teenie was lying impatiently in the bed, waiting for Wullie, whose arthritis was making his disrobing a little slow.

'Oh, me, Wullie,' said Teenie sadly. 'I mind fan we got mairriet; ye hardly gied me time ti tak aff ma stockins. Noo I could near wyve a pair.'

A FARMER became fed up with the state his wife kept the wee bit of garden they had round the farmhouse and found himself inveigled into tidying it up. Since he felt he should be involved in the farm itself, this irked quite a bit.

One day, when the weed problem had got out of hand yet again, he decided the time had come to put his foot down.

'Na, na, na,' he stormed at his wife, 'ti hell wi this. If ye let the gairden get intil a sotter lik this again, I'll gie't a damnt gweed splash o weedkiller.'

'A'richt,' said his wife, 'and I wid jist start pittin yer fool draa'ers til the cleaners.'

... and from *Anither Dash o Doric*

STRAE-RICK fun and frolics involving Elsie and Dode, from two small villages in Banffshire, had led to Elsie's *condition*, although Dode denied it vehemently.

A week after the birth, Elsie's family called a meeting to resolve the matter. On Elsie's side were mother, father and a host of glowering relatives. The only support Dode could muster was his steadfast, loyal younger brother, Wullie.

According to our informant, Wullie was a smiling, open-faced taakin kine o a loon, willing to perjure himself completely in Dode's defence. Why, had the two of them not been in each other's company miles and miles away from the alleged romps on the evening in question.

Alas for Dode.

Steadfast brother Wullie took one look at the innocent in the pram, beamed at the little smiling facie, then turned sadly to Dode and said:

'Oh, Dode, ye canna deny that.'

BILL MOWAT turned up at his Peterhead local with his arm in a sling. The regulars looked him up and down and demanded to know how the accident had happened.

'If ye must ken,' said Bill, 'it got broke fechtin for a lassie's honour.'

'Is that so?'

'Aye, she wintit ti keep it.'

FROM DONSIDE comes the tale of a family who travelled en masse in 1990 to the Leicestershire wedding of one of the young men of their family, who had fallen in love with the English sweetheart he had met at university there.

The wedding was a fairly lavish affair (marquees on the lawn, vol-au-vents, horse-drawn landaulettes – that sort of thing) because, after all, the bride's family was paying. Not only that, but the bride and her family had requested that the ceremony and service be conducted as a 12th-century Eucharist. The obscurity lent it even more elan.

Our Donsiders felt a little out of their depth and, anxious not to show up their boy, had decided to say as little as possible. They had also warned their eight-year-old daughter, something of a tomboy, that discipline would be swift and merciless if she stepped out of line.

Ranks of guests in their finery filled every available pew, and they spanned the entire age spectrum, from grisly matriarchs scowling about them; to rosy-cheeked, avuncular men; to snuffly, emotional mothers, aunties and sisters, and to a brace of under-10s, obviously warned to be on their best behaviour.

There sat the children, faces scrubbed and shining; hair slicked and styled to impossible perfection, dangling their little feet and scarcely concealing their boredom.

A hush fell on the congregation as the organ music died away and the ceremony began. Solemn words echoed to the magnificent rococo ceilings. As the vows were taken, hankies began appearing quietly in various pews.

The couple knelt before the vicar for the blessing, and the silence thickened until it was almost unbearable. It was punctuated only by a very small, impatient North-east voice demanding:

'Is this fin he pits his pollen in her?'

OUR INFORMANT wasn't able to provide hard evidence, but she said with an admirably straight face that a fund-raising cookbook for a notable Buchan church contains the line:

'Many people are obsessed with turnips, and I am married to one.'

AGGIE AND Sandy, from a craftie not a million miles from Lonmay, had been together forty-five years when Sandy retired from his life as a farm-worker. It was to be a big upheaval for Sandy, who was set in his ways. The same would have applied, presumably, to Aggie, having been left on her own for most of the days.

A neighbour ventured to ask as to how she was looking forward to retirement.

'Ach,' she said, 'it'll jist mean twice as muckle o the man and half the siller.'

WE'RE INDEBTED to Duncan Downie, of Kemnay, for this one.

In the village, there lived a well-known spinster by the name of Suffie. We go back to the days when gas lamps were the standard lighting on the bicycles that took you everywhere – especially to village dances at night.

To get a click, it was a ploy of the local belles to ask the lad of their fancy if he had a light to get her gas lamp going. Alas, not for Suffie, as she moaned realistically:

'Plenty spunks. Nivver a lad.'

JIM McCOLL, of Beechgrove Garden fame, contributed this wee gem. The village in question was overloaded with licensed premises and so the publicans had to use their wits to see which one could attract the most business.

Round the village went the rumour that Airchie was seeking planning permission for a nightclub, complete with scantily dressed models.

Annie and Maggie got claikin.

'I hear it said that Airchie's applyin for change o use til a brothel.'

'Michty, Annie, if he canna mak siller sellin drink, he'll nae mak it sellin soup.'

WE'RE NOW in the picture house at Ballater in the late 1940s, and there's a young couple in the back row. It was the time that the travelling cinema shows toured the country areas with such black-and-white epics as *Laurel and Hardy in Bonnie Scotland* and the continuing sagas of *Flash Gordon*.

From the back row, there came this conversation.

'Div ye still love me, Wullie?'

'Aye. I still love ye.'

'Are ye sure ye still love me, Wullie?'

'Aye, I'm sure I still love ye, Jeannie.'

'Fit wye div ye nivver tell me ye love me, Wullie?'

'Look, I really love ye, a'richt?'

'Wullie, if ye still really love me, fit wye div ye nivver ficher wi me noo?'

TAM AND Kirstie lived in a remote glen round about Tomintoul. Every evening, as young lovers did, Tam came to call and they would go for a walk up the glen. This daily ritual had gone on for fourteen years, but there was still no word of matrimony.

So it was on this particular evening that the moon was full and the air warm and soft – a night just made for lovers. And Kirstie, as they say, 'fell from grace'.

Returning down the glen, not a word was spoken, but when they reached the gate of her cottage, Kirstie could contain herself no longer. 'Tam,' she said in a voice filled with emotion. 'Ye'll be thinkin I'm jist a common hooer.'

Clearly alarmed, Tam replied: 'Na, na, Kirstie, there wis nivver ony mention o siller.'

AUL DODDIE, who stayed on a craftie near Muir of Fowlis in the mid-Sixties, was enjoying a dram with his cronies in the lounge of the Muggarthaugh Hotel discussing, among other things, the merits of a shapely young customer, resplendent in a micro mini-skirt.

Noticing the fair bit of attention Doddie was giving the exposed thighs, the proprietor asked what was going through his mind.

'I wis jist thinkin,' said Doddie, 'that fin the Gweed Lord taen awa the ability, fit wye did he nae tak awa the inclination?'

IT WAS the night of the Lonach Gathering, and the Colquhonnie Hotel was fully booked as far as bedrooms were concerned, and fair bursting at the seams with the day's revellers.

All appeared quiet on lights-out an hour or two after last orders, and the homeless stragglers were offered a shak-doon in the residents' lounge.

One particular young lady had been the life and soul of the party and had much impressed the young, hot-blooded lads o Lonach, who now found they shared the same accommodation.

Now resting in deep sleep draped over the settee, our temptress and husband lay to full exposure. One lad more adventurous than the others fancied he would give her a goodnight bosie.

The restless husband stirred, saw the attention of the young chiel and said: 'Hey min, it's me that dis the interficherin roon here.'

DUNCAN DOWNIE, of Kemnay, told of characters in his village, principally two sisters, Mary and Sophia Adam. Both were single and Mary predeceased Suffie by a few years.

Mr Downie Sen. called with his taxi to collect Suffie one evening to go visiting and, as she came out of the house door, she just pulled it shut behind her and didn't bother locking up. Mr Downie drew her attention to what he thought was an oversight.

'Are ye nae lockin yer door?'

'I nivver lock ma door,' replied Suffie.

'Are ye nae feart ye'll find some mannie in the hoose fin ye come back?'

'Nivver been sae lucky.'

JOHN DUFF tells of the Braemar father who watched as his daughter's new boyfriend turned up at the house to take her to a village dance. As they turned to go, he warned the boy: 'Noo dinna blaad the lassie.'

The Shoppie

*The lifeblood of many a small village and hamlet through-
out the North-east was the shoppie – fixed or mobile. Sadly,
these institutions are becoming fewer and farther between,
and even those that remain are losing their character and
the sparkle of wit that crackled back and fore on a good
day. Here are a few remembered fondly.*

THE TRAVELLING fish van is still a feature of North-
east life. Most come from the small fishing ports of the
Moray and Banffshire coasts and ply their trade deep
into the heart of Upper Banffshire, and Central and West
Aberdeenshire.

One morning, at Gartly, the fishman bowled up at one
of his regular customers, who appeared with a stranger at
her side. This turned out to be a visitor from Aberdeen,
and rather a plummy visitor, at that.

When the lady of the house had received her usual order,
the fishman turned his attention to the visitor. 'And fit
aboot you, ma dear?' he inquired.

'Is your fish really fresh?' she said haughtily.

'Really fresh?' he said. 'Look at them!'

Then he turned to the fillets, lying there on a tin tray,
and slapped two or three.

'For God's sake!' he shouted at them. 'I've telt ye afore!
Can ye nae lie still!'

SIGNS in a shop near New Deer. The outside of the door
bears the legend:
   N S Y
The inside of the same door reads:
   S Y OOT

TINKER FAMILIES plied North-east doors for trade as
late as the early 1970s, and one squad was out near Keith
trying to get rid of as many carpet offcuts and, frankly,

moth-eaten fireside rugs as they could. When they stopped at one abode in Moss Street, the lady of the house was having none of it.

'Certainly not,' she said imperiously. 'Michty, yer carpets is stinkin.'

'That's nae the carpets, wifie,' said the tinker. 'That's me.'

ADAM REID was a tailor in Alford. One day in the early 1950s, he told a prominent farmer and church elder who had been fitted for a suit that the suit would be ready in six weeks.

'Sax wikks?' said the farmer. 'That's nae eese ti me; I need it for a waddin in a fortnicht. Michty, it jist took the Lord sax days ti mak the warld.'

'Aye,' said Adam, unimpressed. 'And look at fit a sotter it's in.'

BILL DONALD ran a shop selling, installing and servicing TVs. One day, in the mid-1960s, he took a call from a woman at Glenkindie who was complaining about the quality of her picture.

'Fit exactly's wrang wi yer picter?' he inquired.

'Weel,' said the woman, 'I've the news on aenoo and the blokie readin the news his got an affa lang face.'

'Aye,' said Bill, 'if I wis readin the news nooadays, I wid hae a lang face, tee.'

A BETTERWEAR salesman who had taken a job in the Inverurie area in the 1970s – and is now a prominent Aberdeen businessman – was out in the Garioch trying to drum up trade when he went up to a cottar hoose and knocked sharply. A small boy came to the door.

'Hullo, ma wee lad. Is your mummy in?'

The boy shook his head.

'Is your daddy in?'

The boy shook his head again.

'Well, is there anyone else in that I could speak to?'

The small boy nodded and said. 'Ma sister.'

'OK, can I speak to her?'

So the small boy trotted back into the house and was gone for fully five minutes. Then the boy returned alone and said: 'I canna lift her oot o the playpen.'

A SHOPKEEPER at Banff who happened also to be a prominent after-dinner speaker along the Moray Firth coast remembers being overcome at a football-club dinner at Fraserburgh and falling back into his seat. A large crowd gathered round about him and, in his daze, he remembers hearing them clamouring: 'Move back! Move back!'

He also remembers the wife of one of the club officials shouting: 'Gie him some whisky! Gie him some whisky!'

Others began shouting: 'He needs air! He needs air!'

But still the woman insisted: 'Gie him some whisky! Gie him some whisky!'

Up went shouts of: 'Get an ambulance! Get an ambulance!'

And still the woman insisted: 'Gie him some whisky! Gie him some whisky!'

'Eventually,' he said, 'I raised my head and said: "For ony sake, will somebody listen til the wumman?"'

AN ABERDONIAN who had been imprisoned in Singapore during the war returned to the Granite City after being repatriated and decided that the first thing he wanted to do was to buy himself the bottle of whisky he had dreamed about for so many years in captivity.

At that time, whisky was still in short supply and could be sold only in licensed grocers and pubs within stated licensing hours. A man who had been a prisoner of the Japanese for so many years was a little out of touch with the new customs and went into a back-street Aberdeen grocer who had one bottle of whisky on display in his window.

The PoW went in and said that he wanted to buy the bottle.

'Ye canna buy it,' said the young man, mindful of the licensing laws. 'It's nae 'oors.'

'Well,' said the mystified PoW, 'if it's not yours, why have you got it in your window?'

MAGGIE AND Bessie were two sisters, both now deceased, who were among the most colourful characters in the Howe of Alford. Having been invited to a wedding, Bessie made a rare visit to the hairdresser and announced that she wanted 'the works'.

Worried that an old lady might be alarmed at having to lean backwards over the sink to have her hair washed, the hairdresser asked thoughtfully: 'Wid ye like the back wash for yer hair, Bessie?'

Bessie glared at her.

'The back wash? I'm needin the hale lot washed!'

MAD COW Disease has frightened too many North-east butchery customers for the liking of the trade or of beef farmers, most of whom blame the media for blowing a problem into an epidemic.

One well-known Inverurie lady visited one of the town butchers early in 1993 and was greeted by the usual cheery voice from behind the counter.

'Weel, Mrs Mc——, fit'll it be the day? The usual bit silverside for yer broth?'

'Damn the linth wi yer silverside,' snapped the customer. 'I've heard a aboot this Mad Coo Disease. Keep yer silverside. I'll hae a pun o mince.'

THE SAME butcher reports his experience with a very difficult customer, known with shopkeepers throughout the town for finding fault with everything. There wasn't a please in her.

The butcher had employed a new apprentice and was interested to see how the young lad would cope with Mrs

Difficult. He gave the lad no warning when, as usual, she turned up for her Thursday morning bit of brisket and a hen for the broth.

'Hmm,' she said, peering at the chicken the lad had offered her. 'That disna look affa fresh. It's a bit scrawny. Hiv ye nae nithing better?'

The lad said that that was the last hen they had in stock until later that day. Mrs Difficult asked to see the hen again, and peered at it all the harder, from every angle.

'Ye can see fit I mean, I'm sure,' she said. 'Its skin's a slack and there's nae muckle meat on it.' She leaned a bit closer and sniffed. 'And I'm nae sure bit fit it's on the turn.'

The butcher says he could hardly control his pleasure when the lad said: 'And could ye stand the same inspection yersel?'

A CULLEN fisher couldn't get rid of a sore throat, so his wife went down to Balfour the Chemist for some pastilles or similar soothers. The chemist recommended a particular brand and gave the wife instructions to dissolve one tablet in the mouth as required.

She was back at the chemist within the hour.

'Excuse me, cheemist,' she said, 'dis he swalla the bree?'

JOHN MUSTARD had the souter's shop (shoemaker) at Cullen a few years back and was working away in his back shop one day when he was surprised to see at the counter a young lad asking if he could come and see his father in a hurry.

John knew of the family, but he was not well-acquainted with them. Whatever, he decided he had better do as he had been bidden and see what the problem was. He left his brother in charge of the shop and set off with the wee lad.

It was a wasted journey. The boy had been following instructions from his father, who had been about to sit down to his tea and had told his son: 'Awa and get me mustard.'

AN ABERCHIRDER shop assistant was heard discussing how hard it was to get by on a shop assistant's salary and was drawing much sympathy and empathy from one elderly customer, who said: 'I ken fit it's like. In my young day, I'd an affa job makkin ends meet.'

'I'm nae sae much worriet aboot makkin the ends meet,' said the girl, 'though it wid be real fine if they could get close enough ti wave at een anither noo and again.'

LONG BEFORE the days when we all became so sophisticated, and we all believed in the healing powers of the weird and wonderful cures hawked round the doors by quack doctors, one tinker was plying his trade round homes at Stonehaven, trying to sell bottles of so-called hair-restorer.

Ethel Baird, now of Kincorth, wrote to tell us that her mother had gone to the door to be confronted with the salesman and was not slow to point out that if his hair restorer was so marvellous, why did he not use some of it himself, for he was as bald as a ladle. 'It's a funny salesman that doesn't use his own product.'

Without dallying, the tinker replied: 'Aye, but why should I? Hugh Ramsay (the town draper) sells corsets.'

. . . and from *Anither Dash o Doric*

IN THE early 1970s, when the North-east was gripped with freezer fever, it became fashionable to buy beef in bulk.

One Turriff carnivore phoned Johnny Stewart, the Portsoy butcher, to inquire about freezer packs.

After all the essentials about quantities, cuts and price had been sorted out, the Turriff man asked: 'And do you deliver?'

'Michty, aye,' replied the butcher. 'We dee a kinds o beef.'

MARY GERRIE had promised her grandson a computer for his eighteenth birthday if he managed to gain acceptance to university. Realising she had better price a few computers in case he succeeded in his part of the bargain, she took herself along to a store in Union Street, Aberdeen and, completely out of her depth with technology, began scouting round the computer section.

Having perused all the price tags, she spied one which she thought looked nacky and began pushing a few buttons to see what it would do. All she could get out of it was a high-pitched beeping.

Eventually, a salesman hurried across and asked her, rather abruptly, what she was doing.

'I've promised ma grandson a computer for his birthday,' she said, 'and I canna get this thing ti work ata.'

'Jist as weel,' said the salesman. 'That's wir till.'

THE SCENE was Asda, Dyce, and a harassed young mum Karen Buchan, from Fyvie, had turned up on a busy Saturday morning with two pre-school children in tow to do the monthly shop.

Halfway round, Karen noticed that she was being followed very closely by an elderly gentleman. Whenever she turned into another aisle, he turned into the aisle. Whenever she picked up speed, he picked up speed.

Since you can never be too careful, Karen decided that she had better find a member of staff and had just spotted a shelf-stacker when the elderly gentleman finally caught up with her and stopped her. Karen felt a flash of panic.

'Excuse me,' he said, mildly out of breath. 'Wid it be OK if I got ma trolley back?'

AS DISCUSSED in Volume One, Bessie and Maggie were

two Alford spinsters, now sadly deceased, who lived a spartan existence on the eastern edge of the howe.

Once a week, Bessie would arrive at the Whitehouse Shop and shove a tray or two of eggs at the shopkeeper. He would inspect them; they would agree a price, and Bessie would ram the money into the pocket of her coat and leave.

Now and again, the shopkeeper would scan the eggs and say jokingly: 'Aye, Bessie, yer eggs is nae affa clean the day.'

And a sharp, wiry hand would shoot out from the coat, snatch an egg and hold it up close to her glasses for inspection.

The result was always the same. Bessie would lick the egg, spit on it, rub it up and down the lapel of her coat and ram it back into the cardboard tray and stare sharply at the grocer, defying him to find any more fault with her produce.

He never did.

ONCE, BESSIE happened to bump into a customer who knew the provenance of the duck's eggs. 'Excuse me, Bessie,' said the customer, 'bit I believe you supply the Whitehoose Shop wi dyeuck eggs?'

'I div that,' said Bessie.

'Well, I'm sorry ti say that I hid een recently and it wis rotten.'

'Ach,' said Bessie with a dismissive wave of the hand. 'Canna dee nithing aboot that. That wis the wye the dyeuck laid it.'

NOW WE turn to the art of coiffeur, although in certain parts of the North-east the short back and sides is still referred to as a 'bowl crop'.

Doug Argo, a weel-kent farmer from the Howe o the Mearns, was in need of a haircut and, being a busy man, had not too much time to spare.

In he went to his local barber at Edzell where – changed days – a young lady would attend to the surplus of thatch.

Doug sat himself down and was soon lost in his own thoughts of the day ahead.

Snip snip went the shears until the young lady said something which our Douglas barely heard above the birr of the machine.

'Oh,' replied Doug, 'aboot half wye atween Fettercairn and Auchenblae.'

Our farmer friend thought that she had said: 'Where do you do your farming?'

No wonder the young hairdresser doubled up in laughter; what she had actually said was:

'Where do you have your parting?'

THE YEAR was 1934 and J.O. McHardy had just been promoted to grocer's vanman, entrusted with the 1922 Model T Ford.

This elevation saw him in all kinds of weather, taking in the whole countryside around Wardhouse of Insch.

In the spring of the following year, there was a glut of hens' eggs and, with the guile of which country folk are bred, the decision was made to buy for nothing more than 'saxpince the dizzen'.

J.O. set out on his Friday run which took in, as usual, the farm of Sleepytoun.

The farmer's wife, a good-hearted soul, was told the price being offered for her eggs and replied:

'Laddie, it's nae worth the craters raxin for't.'

BAIRNS AT Woodside, Aberdeen, made sure that the route to the corner shoppie was well used. Bargains were to be had, of course, and aul Andra, the shopkeeper, aye had a pocketful of rather grubby pandrops to entice the youngsters on to other wares.

The handing-over of the pandrop was always accompanied by:

'Jist spit oot the first sook.'

ON A visit to Strathdon, Ian Middleton, from near Buckie, went into the shop and asked for a new type of chocolate bar he had seen advertised on TV.

'Could I hae a Topic, please?' he inquired, to which he got the answer:

'Affa sorry, loon. I've jist the Dandy and the Beano.'

ACCORDING TO our informant, Granny took young Tracy to shop for a wedding gift at Makro, the Dutch-owned wholesale superstore newly set-up in Aberdeen. She made for the crystal display and was taken with a rosebowl complete with silver mesh.

'This'll dee, I'm sure,' said Granny, keeping the youngster occupied.

'Oh I ken fit at's for, Grunny,' said Tracy.

'Fit?' said Granny, wondering what was coming.

'Breein cubbidge.'

Down on the Farm

Although you would never think so to listen to them, some of the best of North-east humour comes from farming circles, particularly once the farmers get together socially, and any non-farmer who manages to inveigle himself into their company is assured an entertaining few hours.

AT A DINNER held by the National Farmers' Union in Aberdeen, and attended by some of the wealthiest tillers of the soil the North-east of Scotland can boast, the guests were not greatly impressed by the after-dinner speaker – a dull, wordy and not particularly entertaining councillor.

A Huntly farmer leaned to the man on his right and said: 'I've nivver really heard an efter-dinner speech worth listenin til. Hiv you?'

'Michty aye,' said the other. 'Last wikk, I wis oot wi the bunker and he said: "I'll pey the bill."'

A VET near Inverurie had been attending the very difficult birth of a calf. The labour had taken most of the night and everyone in attendance – vet, farmer, wife and son – was exhausted.

Finally, at six in the morning, just as the farmer's youngest son, aged seven, appeared in the doorway, the calf fell on to the straw to a great cacophony of mooing from the proud mother, and sighs of relief and tiredness from the four humans.

The farmer's eldest son, leaning on a byre post, exhausted, said: 'Fit is't?' – meaning was the newborn male or female, for in all the excitement they had been too busy to take note.

The small boy who had just appeared was standing by and said shyly: 'Gies a look at the calfie. I ken foo ye can tell.'

A FARM labourer convicted of lewd behaviour involving a

cow had been fined at Banff Sheriff Court and – somewhat unwisely, it must be said – had decided to visit a café in the town for his lunch before returning to the farm.

Without a word, a waitress appeared and laid in front of him a plate of carrot tops, oatmeal, grass and dockens.

He stared at the plate and looked up at her, incredulous. 'Fit's this?' he demanded. 'I canna aet this.'

'No?' she said. 'Well, if you canna, jist gie it til yer girlfriend.'

A FARMER had been refused planning permission for a new house for his son, and so had to resort to finding a cottage somewhere near Rothienorman. He had inquired with all the nearby farmers to see if they had anything spare that they might sell, but none had.

Eventually, he took his son to see an estate agent at Inverurie, but everything on the agent's books was either too far away, too big or, more often, too expensive.

By the time they came to the last property on file, the farmer took off his bunnet, sighed, and ran a hand through his hair. 'Lord,' he said. 'Hiv ye nithing for aboot twa thoosan?'

'I'm sure,' said the estate agent. 'Come oot wi me the morn's mornin and we'll see if it's still stannin.'

A PROMINENT farming family in Aberdeenshire (whom we won't name because they are still in situ) were mildly resented in the nearby community for the way they spent their money in what the townsfolk judged was the flashiest way possible. The family's children, according to local opinion, were indulged right from birth to the time each made its own way in the world.

When the business venture of one collapsed, it became the speak of the place, particularly at the mart, where one farmer observed drily: 'Life hisna been easy for young ——. He'll ken aboot problems noo that it's a collapsed roon aboot his heid.'

'Aye,' said the other. 'Problems, richt enough. I doot he'll jist hae ti grit his teeth, roll up his sleeves and ask his faither for anither fifty thoosan.'

THE GREAT drought of 1976 reduced virtually all the North-east farming population to despair, to such a degree that one Ellon minister prayed from the pulpit for rain. On the Monday, one of the most violent thunderstorms in years drenched the area and ruined a large acreage of what crops existed.

'And that's the trouble wi the meenister,' one farmer announced to another at the mart later that week. 'He aye overdis things.'

A FORMER lecturer at the North of Scotland College of Agriculture in Aberdeen swears that this story, from the early 1960s, is true. A chicken farmer near Laurencekirk was losing a lot of his stock, despite the intervention of vets, and decided as a last resort to write to the college to see if they had any advice.

'Every morning, when I go out, I find two or three more lying on the ground, cold and stiff, with their legs in the air. Can you tell me what is the matter?'

A few days later, he received a reply: 'Dear Mr ——. Your hens are dead.'

A FORMER waitress at the Northern Hotel, Kittybrewster, Aberdeen, wrote to us and sought anonymity for her tale from the days when the biggest mart in the North of Scotland was held every Friday just a few hundred yards along the road from the hotel, and farmers from five counties and beyond converged to do business or just have a news.

One particular Strathbogie farmer was a notorious twister, who was never slow to try to get something for nothing.

Our waitress recalled him turning up and asking for a plate of mince and tatties. This was duly served him but, before he started tucking in, he asked if he could change his mind and have a plate of the steak-and-kidney pie, instead. The waitress obliged; removed the mince and tatties, and returned five minutes later with the pie, which he ate hungrily.

He stood up and was walking out when the waitress caught him near the front door and reminded him that he hadn't paid.

'Aye, aye, lassie, bit if I mind richt I gied ye a plate o mince and tatties for the steak-and-kidney pie, did I nae?'

'Well, yes, but you didn't pay for the mince and tatties.'

'Bit I didna aet the mince and tatties, so fit wye should I pey for it?'

THE DRAM after paying the hairst bill is a custom throughout the North-east, and probably far beyond. One farmer's wife from near Oyne told us of the evening in the late 1970s when the combine-owner had called to seek his due and her man had reached for the bottle of Grouse to seal the deal.

Both men sat down, but the visitor was looking into the dram very glumly.

'Is there something adee?' inquired the farmer.

'There's a flee in ma dram, min,' said the visitor.

'Oh, I'm sorry aboot that,' said the farmer's wife, stepping in to retrieve the glass.

'Na, na,' said the visitor, pulling the glass back closer to himself. 'I'm nae bothered aboot the flee – jist the wye it's widin across the boddim.'

A CROFTER from Craigievar paid an evening visit to a neighbouring farm. The crofter had spent most of his life as a cattleman on various farms, breeding Aberdeen-Angus and Shorthorn cattle.

On being asked into the farmhouse for a fly cup, the

conversation between the two men inevitably was of pedigree cattle.

After a considerable time, the farmer's wife felt the need to change the subject of the conversation and tried to steer it round by asking the crofter how his niece was getting on now that she had gone to Aberdeen to work.

'Deein gran,' said the crofter. 'She's got a job as a shorthorn-typist.'

TWO CROFTER brothers were drying off at the fireside in their wee hoose after a pouring wet day in the fields.

'I winder if the rain's stoppit yet,' said one.

'Dinna ken,' said the other. 'I hinna been oot since I come in.'

IN THE 1990s, it is known as 'an insurance job', but several decades ago no one could be so openly suspicious of a neighbour or friend, least of all in the farming community, but there were ways and ways.

A fire broke out in one Buchan farmer's strae-ricks early one morning, and a troupe of neighbours turned out to do what they could to douse the flames, but to little effect.

The farmer stepped away, looking extremely calm, took out his pipe and lit his tobacco. One of his exhausted neighbours turned to him.

'Weel, weel, Geordie,' he said. 'I doot that's nae the first time yer spunks hiv been oot the day.'

WE HAD better keep the names here secret, but the story involves a farmer near Dunecht, whose farm was being inspected by a representative of the Ministry of Agriculture. Being invited into the farmhouse, the ministry man said he would be delighted to meet Mrs G——.

'Aweel,' said the farmer, 'come awa in. I hinna a bonnie wife, bit I can show ye some real bonnie coos.'

JUST BEFORE the end of World War I, a group of Garioch

farmers were at the mart discussing what punishment would be suitable for the Kaiser for all the havoc, death and destruction he and his like had wrought.

Many punishments were dreamed up, each more vicious than the one before, but they fixed on what they thought was the best of the lot.

They would give him an overdraft on a small, north-facing croft at Rhynie.

WE DEBATED long and hard over whether or not to include this one at all, for it is easily the least tasteful story in the book, but on the grounds that North-east people are not easily shockable, it is included. We won't embarrass the contributor by naming him. If you are easily shockable yourself, close your eyes now.

A Peterhead farmer went into the chemist in 1962 for a packet of condoms, 'Foo muckle's that?' he inquired.

'One pound, plus tax,' said the assistant.

'Nivver mind the tacks,' he said. 'I'll jist tie them on wi binder twine.'

THE DAYS of the travelling threshing-mill round the crofts showed North-east community spirit at its best, with neighbour helping neighbour. At dinnertime or teatime, the small living room of the croft being hairstit would be full to overflowing.

Always, two men would arrive the night before with the steam mill so that they could set it up in fine time for an early yokin the following morning.

At this particular croft, the two steam-mill men were not known to the crofter's wife, but she was mindful of her duty in making sure that they felt welcome when they arrived for their meal.

'Aet up stem-mull man,' she said. 'Aet up at man aside ye.'

IT HAD been a particularly boring football match at

Pittodrie. The Dons certainly had not been at their best, and the final whistle blew with the scoresheet blank.

A group of Kemnay farm workers was making a slow, dejected exit, when one looked at another and said: 'We'd hiv been as weel at hame githerin steens.'

IT HAD been a most enjoyable day at the sheepdog trials at Monymusk. The competitions were over and the post-mortems had to be conducted over a sociable dram. This meant that Dod stayed longer than he had intended, and all thoughts of the raging wife at home had long since evaporated.

It wasn't until he was dropped off at the end of the road that he began to panic. We didn't discover what happened next until the following sheepdog trial when Dod, fortified with the barley bree again, explained.

His wife, apparently, had gone to bed already by the time he had got home. He crept upstairs as slowly and as quietly as his delicate state would allow. He had just reached the top of the stairs and had pushed open the door gently when his wife stirred.

'I jist crawlt in on all fours til the bedside,' said Dod, 'and the wife pit oot her haun, sayin: "Is that you, Flossie?" '

'Did ye get aff wi't, Dod?' inquired a crony.

'I did,' said Dod. 'I hid the presence o mind ti lick her haun.'

TWO Oldmeldrum farmers had met at the local smiddy in the late 1950s. One was known to be very young, thrusting and ambitious, with an eye to maximum pro-ductivity and new methods. The other was of the old school.

Passing the time of day while the smith attended to their needs, the younger was heard to remark that he was planning to erect a massing building on his land. It would be hundreds of yards long and hundreds of yards wide and a good few yards in height. It would be one of the grandest buildings in the Garioch. And what scope it would give him once it was finished.

After he had finished telling of his plans, he waited for the older farmer to be suitably admiring, but the reply was:

'Aye, aye, aye. Bit far I come fae we like ti ploo a bit o the grun, an a.'

MANY YEARS ago, there was a particularly impressive bull at Tarland, which gave the farmer immense pride and, in truth, caused a lot of admiration around the Howe of Cromar. One day, the minister called and asked if he might see this bull that everyone was talking about and the farmer agreed readily and began walking towards a nearby field.

'Oh,' said the minister, 'I had assumed it would be safely locked up in a stall, where I could see it at close quarters.'

'Na, na, meenister,' said the farmer. 'It's oot in the park.'

The minister followed, a little more reluctantly, and soon saw the massive animal, standing alone in the centre of a field. He swallowed a little.

The farmer stopped beside the gate and bade the minister jump in over. The minister clambered in over with a little difficulty and waited for the farmer to join him. But the farmer stayed where he was, leaning on the outside of the gate.

'Are you not coming, too?' inquired the minister.

'Na, na,' said the farmer. 'I ken fit he looks like. I've seen him plenty o times. Awa ye go.'

The minister thought for a moment, summoned his courage and began stepping gingerly towards the centre of the park. Half-way, he stopped, turned and said: 'What if he charges?'

'He winna charge,' said the farmer. 'Ye dinna think I'd pit ye in there yersel if he wis the kinna bull that charged.'

'No, but just supposing he does charge. What do I do?'

'Weel,' said the farmer. 'I wid turn roon, pick up a handfae and fling it at him.'

'A handful of what?'

'Dinna worry,' said the farmer. 'It'll be there.'

. . . and from *Anither Dash o Doric*

BUNKIE PETRIE, a celebrated Aberdeenshire farmer, used to tell a story of two farmers at the old Alford mart taking everyone and everything through haun when an extremely glamorous young woman, dolled up to the nines and made up and bejewelled most elegantly, strolled into the mart building, obviously for a look at how the other half lived.

'Michty,' said one farmer to the other. 'Fit wid ye dee wi a deemie lik that?'

His companion surveyed her with the steady eye of Aberdeenshire farming stock.

'Na, Bill,' he said. 'If it needs a that tap-dressin, it maun be gey sair grun aneth.'

BUCHAN MEAT, one of the great farming organisations of Scotland, had a rocky 1996, suffering great financial uncertainty, partly to do with the BSE crisis. There was one little glimmer of North-east humour at a creditors' meeting, attended by farmers and shareholders from throughout Buchan and beyond.

One journalist assigned to cover the meeting was growing more and more anxious about the likely finishing time because he had another pressing engagement. He turned to the chap standing next to him and whispered:

'Excuse me, but have you any idea what time this meeting might finish?'

The chap whispered back in broad Buchan: 'Ten ti fower.'

Since the meeting at that stage looked to be reaching its

angry pitch, and it was already 3.35 p.m., the journalist was puzzled by the certainty and precision.

'That's very precise,' he whispered back. 'How can you be so sure?'

The helpful chap pointed across the assembly to a lone figure in dungars and requisite farmer's bunnet. 'Ye see that chiel ower there?' he said. 'That's Dode. Dode starts his milkin at fower.'

RETIRED KEITH vet John Dear told of the day, shortly after his arrival from Hampshire in 1961, when he was called out to see a sow with a problem. When he asked the old-lady smallholder what was the difficulty, she said: 'Ma soo's nae takkin her mate.'

Mr Dear began discussing possible fertility problems and wondered whether or not the sow was being presented properly to the boar.

The old woman glared at him and said: 'No, no, no. She's nae takkin her *maet*. Her maet. She's nae *aetin*.'

MR DEAR also told of an incident at the other end of his career, not long before his retirement, when he was called to a farmer who had reported several head of cattle with several sore eyes, or one beast with one sore eye, it was not quite clear from the phone message.

When he arrived, Mr Dear asked the farmer about the scale of the problem. Was it several eyes, or just one?

'Oh, aye,' said the farmer. 'Ae ee, aye.'

A RETIRED Maud farmer wrote to tell us of one of his neighbours, who had wed late in life and had supposedly proposed to his bride by saying:

'Is it nae aboot time you an me startit pittin wir teeth in ae cup?'

CHARLIE CHEYNE, who was a mechanic at an agricultural garage in the Howe of Alford in the 1960s and

1970s, used to tell of a farmer's teenage son who turned up one morning with one of the farm tractors looking for an emergency repair. Charlie downed tools to help the lad out and, while Charlie worked, the lad gabbed on and on, mostly about himself, the family farm and all the plans he had for it once his father retired.

'Aye,' said Charlie from the depths of the tractor, 'ye've great dreams surely.'

'Aye, Charlie,' said the lad, brimful of confidence and certainty. 'I dream I'll mak a million poun, jist lik the aul man.'

Charlie stopped. 'Yer faither nivver made a million poun,' he said.

'No,' said the lad, 'bit he's aye dreamin o't.'

DURING THE building of Thainstone Mart, near Inverurie, two Garioch farmers had stopped on their way back from Kittybrewster one Friday to see how construction was going and spotted a group of labourers gathered round watching two of their colleagues laying pipes.

'Look at that,' said Westie, 'ye widna hiv seen that thirty-forty year ago. In my day, the ganger let them lay twa length o pipe, then he turned on the watter. If they didna keep in front o't, they got the sack.'

THE LATE Maitland Mackie, a leading light in North-east local government in his day, used to tell of meeting an Echt farmer during a council site visit and getting newsing about the state of farming, before discovering that they had a mutual farmer acquaintance. The acquaintance's son had had a gweed heid on him, they had agreed, and had been expected to do great things as a doctor or lawyer or some such, but had ended up as a sewerage foreman for the old Aberdeen County Council.

There was a long silence while the two of them considered the lad's choice of career then, said Maitland, the farmer stood up from the fence on which he had been leaning and said: 'Weel, nivver mind, at least he can say he's Number One in Number Two.'

THE FARMER at Balblair was visited by a rather pushy salesman who was determined to sell him a fire-extinguisher.

'It's the latest model and guaranteed for five years. It's absolutely essential for anyone who is concerned about fire safety on his premises.'

'No.'

'For a very small investment you can have absolute peace of mind and be free to concentrate on other things.'

'No.'

'All forward-thinking farmers are realising that with so many flammable materials round the farm, a reliable fire extinguisher is essential these days.'

'No.'

'B-but what would you do if you had a fire and you didn't have one of our extinguishers?'

'Pish on't.'

IN THE early days of deep-litter hens, Jock Anderson had decided to give the new system a try. Bumping into him one day, his fairmer pal Doug Archibald asked how the hens were doing.

'Nae layin worth a damn. I'm nae happy wi them. I'm takkin them aff o the pellets – ower damnt dear. I'll try a mash o bruised corn and sma tatties.'

Seeing Jock a few weeks later, Doug was anxious to know how the hens were laying on their new diet.

'Nae worth a bugger,' said Jock. 'Nithing bit barrafaes o shite.'

A FARMER from Newburgh who was a most infrequent member of the village golf club was persuaded by a major fertiliser company to be a guest for a day's outing to St. Andrews.

The main hazards at Newburgh were only whin bushes, and he was totally unprepared for the obstacles awaiting him at the home of golf. Visiting one of the notorious bunkers out of sight of his partners, he was in deep trouble.

A plaintive cry went out after he had been in the same sand trap for about ten minutes: 'Help. I canna win oot.'

'Ach,' said his playing partner waiting impatiently up the fairway, 'it's just a friendly. Throw the ball out and nobody will notice.'

'The ba? The ba? It's *me* that canna win oot.'

IT WAS the same player who, not adhering to the once-bitten-twice-shy maxim, joined yet another firm's outing, this time to Stonehaven. He came to the nasty ravine over the sea cliffs which is a nightmare for non-golfers. It's only a matter of 120 yards, but from the tee you are required to float the ball over the ravine to the small green at the other side.

Geordie sent one off and it went straight down the cliffs. Then another. And another. And another.

Losing patience completely, he took yet another new ball and set it on the tee still with the wrapper on.

There went another almighty swing with the parting words: 'Tak that, ye bugger. It's nae worth ma file takkin ye oot o the paper.'

A FARMER from Glenkindie was called into the tax office to explain certain deficiencies in his submitted accounts.

The inspector behind the desk said that he wasn't too pleased about his books and queried the fact that although the farmer had lots of cows, there was no record of any milk money.

'What do you do with the milk?' he asked.

'Oh,' said the farmer, 'I sook ma coos.'

'Don't be ridiculous,' snapped the taxman. 'How do you do that?'

'Ye bliddy feel, it's nae me that sooks the coos,' said the farmer. 'It's the caafies.'

DOUG HAMPTON, of Laurencekirk, reminded us of the plans to build a gents' toilet in the Lang Toon in the Thirties. The town paper referred to it as a urinal – a gey uncommon title for the watterie in those days.

At a heckling meeting prior to the district elections, a town worthy known only as Auld Dod got to his feet to ask: 'Far are ye gaun ti pit this arsenal abody's spikkin aboot?'

ANOTHER NOTABLE from the Laurencekirk area, Davie, had a dairy and floating business up beside the Western Hotel. He had about ten cows in the dairy and delivered milk around the town.

He decided it might be more economical to buy a bull and managed to procure a gey old beast, but good enough to sire his cows.

Davie took the first of the calves down to the mart hoping for a good price. When one was introduced to the ring as his, he realised there had been a mix-up.

'That's nae my calf,' he declared, much to the auctioneer's annoyance. Davie, the auctioneer and the mart manager convened a hasty meeting, and the manager insisted that the calf had to be Davie's, for his mart never made mistakes.

Glowering at the auctioneer, Davie shouted: 'Gweed God, I shid ken ma ain calf. I bulled the coo masel.'

A MEARNS farmer who was a bit of a blaw and some bothered with a thirst (so we won't name him because his descendants still farm in the area) was up at the Feein Market in the Castlegate, Aberdeen, during the 1914–18 war. As was the custom, the recruiting sergeants were buzzing around and a few of the lads were home on leave.

A Salvation Army lass came up to our Man o the Mearns

with a collecting tin, to which he responded: 'Fit army are you in, then?'

'The Army of the Lord,' was the lass's reply.

'Weel, ye're a helluva lang wye fae yer barracks.'

IT WAS a National Farmers' Union meeting. Airchie was deaf and was missing most of the content of the speeches.

'Is that mannie aye spikkin?' he bawled into his neighbour's ear.

'Aye, he's aye spikkin,' came the weary reply. 'Bit he's nae sayin onything.'

AUL WILLIE stayed by himself and farmed his land singlehandedly. He had his own system of home economics. A neighbour happened in past and, seeing the clutter on the mantelpiece, asked politely how Willie dealt with paying his bills.

'Ach,' said Willie. 'Fin they come in, I jist stick them ahen the clock.'

'Bit ye must dee something wi them some time.'

'Ay! Fin the clock faas doon.'   .

THE DAY'S sheepdog trials at Monymusk had gone rather well and the winner, Airchie, was being feted left, right and centre at the wee lounge bar out by the village.

A couple from Winnipeg were on holiday. They were from farming stock and had been most impressed.

'Say Archie, I'll give you a thousand dollars for that dog,' said the Canadian.

Airchie made no comment, but a Welsh enthusiast from the dales was also taken by the dog. 'Well sir, I am a keen triallist myself,' he said, 'and I would love that dog, too, but I'm afraid four hundred pounds is my limit.'

The Canadian upped his bid to three thousand and the impassive Airchie was not swayed until later in the evening when, over a few drams, he decided to take the Welshman's offer.

His erstwhile pal, Geordie, said: 'Ye daft bugger. Ye've refused three thoosan dollars an taen the peerer offer. Ye're aff yer heid.'

Puffing his pipe with an air of contentment, Airchie reasoned:

'Weel, kennin Flossie, gin she gets doon the length o Wales, she'll seen win her wye hame, bit I'm damnt sure she'll nae sweem the Atlantic.'

Characters

They say that characters are the fuel on which any region's humour is based. Some say that the fuel is running dry, which seems a thochtie pessimistic to us. Here is proof that the Doric is all the richer for the legacy of its notables, past and present.

BERT DUNCAN, from Woodside, Aberdeen, became celebrated in the shadowy world of London boxing as one of the finest corners a boxer could hope to have supporting him. During one fight, in the mid-1950s, Bert was accompanying a distinctly unimpressive boxer from the dressing-room to the ring.

'It's a long way, isn't it?' said the boxer.

'Dinna worry,' growled Bert. 'Ye winna be walkin back.'

ONE OF the North-east's most celebrated auctioneers is Bill Lippe, whose evenings at Kemnay draw crowds for miles. One evening, the story goes, a handsome stuffed parrot in a large cage appeared. Bidding for Lot 165 began at £10. Bill was surprised that interest took off quite as spectacularly as it did – and certainly far in excess of what he judged the lot was worth.

Finally, just two bidders were in competition with one another: a farmer's wife from Blairdaff and an unknown voice across at the front, right-hand corner of the village hall.

People round about the Blairdaff woman were growing gradually more incredulous that she should be thinking of spending such money on a stuffed parrot, but she had a determined set about her jaw and was clearly intent on winning.

Finally, at £85, the prize was hers and two farmers nearby leaned across to congratulate her. 'Well, Mrs——,' said one. 'At that price, I hope he's a good spikker.'

'Och, he's a rare spikker,' said the other. 'Fa div ye think she wis biddin against?'

PAT BUCHAN, who used to teach dancing around Edinburgh before retiring back to his native Peterhead in the mid-1950s, used to tell of teaching a class of novices at a well-known school for the well-heeled young lady and taking, as a partner, a very nervous and easily embarrassed young deb.

He instructed her to watch his feet carefully and to try to follow everything he did.

She was so desperate to do well that she kept one step ahead of him all the time, without waiting for his lead. After several stops and starts, he admitted to growing a little impatient and eventually stopped, sighed and said: 'I'm sorry, but yer problem is that ye're anticipatin.'

'I am not!' she blushed. 'I'm not even married!'

WILLIE LUMSDEN was a passenger porter at Inverurie Railway Station for almost half a century, a well-kent figure and known to almost everyone who travelled on the line, and certainly to every soul in the Garioch.

He also dabbled as an amateur chiropodist, in days when farmers and farmworkers suffered all manner of problems because their feet were expected to withstand the harshest of winters, the poorest of footwear and the most neglectful of care.

One evening, an unnamed farmworker turned up to have a particularly ugly foot attended to. Willie did the best he could and the client put his sock and boot back on again.

'Oh, what fine, Wullie,' he said, sighing with pleasure. 'I wish noo that I'd washed ma ither fit.'

MAGGIE, A waitress at the former Gloucester Hotel in Union Street, Aberdeen, reports working for one summer season with a country-bred waitress who stood no nonsense from anyone.

When one diner complained that he had detected no hint of oxtail in the oxtail soup, she glared at him, snatched the plate and announced: 'And ye'll be disappintit ti hear there's nae horse in wir horseradish, eether.'

MAGGIE'S COLLEAGUE had been asked to stand in for an afternoon behind reception to cover for a receptionist who had become ill. When one guest approached to ask if he could buy stamps for a parcel, Maggie's colleague raked about among the drawers and found a sheet of stamps.

She tore off the requisite amount and the man pushed the right number of coins across the counter, as well as the parcel. Maggie's colleague's stare told the man that she was not prepared to do anything more for him.

'W-well,' he said, hesitating. 'Will I stick the stamps on myself?'

'Please yersel,' said Maggie's colleague. 'Though ye'd likely be better stickin them on yer parcel.'

THE SAME lady was back in the dining-room and had been confronted by a QC up from Edinburgh who was having a quick lunch during recess from court and who was clearly not impressed with the cuisine and called her over to say so.

'I have a complaint,' he said.

'This is a hotel,' she said, cruising past. 'Nae a hospital.'

IT WAS the night of the Harvest Home dance at the big hoose, when the laird and his entourage mixed with tenants, estate workers, guests and villagers to celebrate the end of the harvest.

In the middle of an eightsome reel, the second horseman, fortified with the dram, engaged the laird in conversation.

'Man, fit a gran nicht. I'm fair conspirin.'

'Conspiring?' queried his lordship. 'Conspiring means "to plot".'

''At's richt, min,' said the horseman. 'I'm fair plottin.'

JOHN DUNCAN, of Dubbieford Farm, near Torphins, enjoyed long and strong friendships in the community and was highly regarded by all who knew him. Jack Kellas, of Torphins, wrote to tell us of a bit news he had once with Dubbie when the subject worked its way round to fenceposts.

Jack offered Dubbie the chance to buy some surplus that he happened to have after buying more than he found he needed.

'Fit like a price wid ye be needin?' inquired Dubbie.

'Twa shillins apiece,' said Jack. 'They're oak. They'll laist for ivver.'

Dubbie rubbed his chin. 'Ah, bit ye're gey strong in the price, Jake. Dam't, ye're needin ower muckle, I'm thinkin.'

Jack thought for a moment. 'Well, fit aboot a shillin each? A real bargain.'

'Weel, ye are saftenin a bittie bit, ach, ye ken, I'm nae sair-needin posts aenoo. Ma fences is real snod.'

'Right, John,' said Jack, 'I'll tell ye fit: ye can hae the twinty posts for nithing. Will that please ye?'

Dubbie grasped him by the shoulder, grinning. 'Now, haud on Jake, haud on,' he said. 'Is that delivered?'

JACK KELLAS tells also of another good neighbour, farmer George Anderson, who was summoned to attend the Inland Revenue office in Aberdeen for an investigation of his accounts. George was reluctant to go, but was persuaded that it would be better in the long run to get the matter cleared up. Not every farmer in those days had a car, but a neighbouring farmer, Hilly, offered to run him into town.

The two set off on Friday morning and, after attending the mart at Kittybrewster, made their way down town to the Inland Revenue office. On arrival, Hilly suggested that he would sit outside in the car while George set about his business with the tax man.

'Na, na,' insisted George. 'Ye're nae sittin oot here

stairvin. Ye'd better come awa in and see fit this bliddy mannie his ti say.'

Once the tax inspector was persuaded that it would be all right for a third party to be present while Mr Anderson's accounts were examined, they set about taking the books through hand.

'Now, Mr Anderson,' said the inspector, poring over sheets of figures. 'I see that at the start of your year you had six hundred head of poultry. Is that correct?'

'Michty aye.'

'And you bought four hundred and fifty during the year?'

'Aye.'

'Well, there is something far wrong here, it seems to me. You have no sales recorded during the year and your closing valuation number is only seven hundred. What happened to the other three hundred and fifty? Do you still have them?'

'No,' said Geordie, becoming a little uncomfortable. 'I hinna.'

'You don't have them?'

'No.'

'So where do you suppose they might be then?'

'I suppose they must hiv dee't.'

'Died? Three hundred and fifty of your poultry have died? What on earth could they have died of?'

Geordie fixed him with a stare.

'The skitter.'

WE'D BETTER not reveal the man's name, but we'll call him Jock the Coalman. A week before Christmas a few years back, the conversation in the village pub got round to finding a bird for the Christmas Day table, and memories of the size of some turkeys they had seen over the years.

Jock listened in silence as one of the worthies continually topped everyone else's stories with a 30-pounder he'd had a few years previously.

'And fit aboot yersel, Jock?' somebody asked. 'Fit's the biggest turkey ee've ivver seen?'

'Weel,' drawled Jock, 'fin I come awa fae the hoose this mornin, the wife wis dressin oor turkey, and it wis that big she wis rowin stuffin up its erse wi a box barra.'

BRYAN SMITH, now of Aberdeen, tells a story from his wartime days in the Far East, much adapted by after-dinner speakers ever since, but this is the original.

It concerns Waddy, third horseman at Drumdelgie, and then in the 9th Battalion Gordon Highlanders. In January, 1945, they were crossing the Irrawaddy when they were divebombed by six Japanese Zero fighters. Mr Smith's batman was shot through the head. Waddy received a leg wound and was removed to a forward casualty-clearing station behind the lines.

Who should appear shortly afterwards but Field Marshal Sir Bill Slim. The great man spotted Waddy, lying there, smoking the ubiquitous stubby pipe so beloved of farm servants between the wars, and wreathed in clouds of XX Bogie Roll. The field marshal bent down and inquired of Waddy: 'Tell me, man, where exactly were you wounded?'

Waddy pondered for a moment, sat up and replied: 'Weel, sir, I jaloose it wid hiv been a twa-three mile the Huntly side o the Irrawaddy.'

THE LATE Jock Strachan was a well-known and well-respected farmer in the Fyvie area. One evening, he turned up at a concert at Fyvie and the compere of the show noticed that Jock was present. Between two of the acts, the compere told the story of a teacher asking her class for definitions of words, and she had asked for a definition of the word Nothing.

A boy had shot up his hand and had said: 'Please, miss, it's fit ye get for haudin Jock Strachan's horse.'

ONE EVENING, a group of Oldmeldrum worthies were discussing the forthcoming Oldmeldrum Sports, that annual gala which is as much a part of North-east culture as the Turriff Show, the Lonach or the Braemar Gathering.

'Ach, I'm nae gyaun this eer,' said Jock. 'It's aye the same. Quines duncin. Bill Anderson throwin his haimmer farrer than the neist lad. Tugga-war. Pipers dirlin a'b'dy's lugs. Nithing new. Na na, nae for me.'

'Oh, bit ye're wrang,' said Sandy. 'For instance, tak the pageant. This year, the theme's Legends Throweoot The Centuries, and I hear say that the Meldrum Rural wifies are gaun as Lady Godiva – ye ken, the wifie that rode throwe the streets bare-nakit, tirred til the skin o a fite horse.'

'Ach,' said Jock, 'maybe I will ging. It's a filie sin I've seen a fite horse.'

WILLIE WEBSTER was the joiner at Methlick and, in the 1950s, was visited by the factory inspector who demanded to see the joinery's fire extinguisher.

'Up in the laft,' said Willie.

The inspector was perplexed, for he could see no stair to the loft. 'Mr Webster, how do I get up there?'

'Use a laidder.'

Willie produced a ladder and the inspector proceeded, shakily, into the loft, where he found the extinguisher under a pile of old sacks – hardly the most accessible point in case of emergency.

But, worse, it was empty.

'Of coorse it's impty,' snapped Willie. 'If I kept it full, it wid jist roost.'

'And what would you do if there was a fire?'

'Fill it, of coorse.'

AT INSCH Station, one gate of the level crossing was shut, but the other was left open. Peter Scatterty, on duty as signalman, was asked by Harry Usher what was going on.

'Well,' said Peter. 'I'm half-expectin a train.'

AT A major Fiddlers' Spectacular at HM Theatre, Aberdeen,

there was an age gap of 85 years between the youngest and the oldest of the 100 assembled musicians – the youngest was nine and the oldest, Harry Nicol, of Cults, a mere 94.

After a day-long dress rehearsal before the week's show, Harry went into his local at the Ploughman, Culter, for a wee dram to ease away the other elbow exertions on the stage. His trusty fiddle was in its case under his arm as he made his way to the bar. The proprietor greeted him with: 'Michty, Harry, far hiv ye been?'

'I've been awa for a practice,' said Harry.

'Michty,' said mine host, 'at your age, min, if ye canna play the damnt thing afore this time, it's hardly worth yer file yokin.'

IN THE mid-1960s, BBC Scotland staged a grand fiddle concert at Blair Castle, home of the Duke of Atholl. The concert featured fiddlers from throughout Scotland and producer James Hunter had persuaded noted virtuoso Yehudi Menuhin to take part. Menuhin was, and still is, most appreciative of the Scottish style of fiddle-playing, but expressed reservations on being able to handle the technique at short notice.

Some of the fiddlers on stage, to put it mildly, were more enthusiastic than expert, and so it was at rehearsal that the guest was shown a seat between two elderly fiddlers of rural stock, who fitted in well in strathspey-and-reel circles, but never professed to being individual stars.

'Gentlemen,' said Menuhin, 'thanks for the honour, but I must confess to being a little apprehensive and nervous in following your music.'

'Nivver ee mind, chiel,' said the lad on his right. 'Ye're atween twa gweed men.'

NO TRUE man or woman of the North-east has not heard of Jamie Fleeman. The Laird O Udny's Feel, as he was known, was born in 1723 and spent most of his working life as manservant to the Laird of Udny Castle in Aberdeenshire. He was of simple mind, but his loyalty to the laird was staunch, although he often despised the laird's friends, perhaps because they thought they could get away with poking sarcastic jibes at 'the fool', but it was Jamie who always got the better of them, and the stories are legend.

One of the landed gentry had been a guest of Udny and had made some remark that had upset Jamie. Revenge came the next morning as Jamie was having a wee snooze on the banks of the Ythan when the guest appeared at the other side of the river with his horse.

He shouted across and asked Jamie where the best crossing-point would be. Jamie directed him to the deepest bit of the water. The gentleman urged his horse in and both promptly disappeared. The gentleman nearly drowned.

Spitting with rage, and utterly drenched, he hauled himself back out on to the bank and shouted that Jamie had tried to kill him.

'Gweed be here,' cried Jamie, 'I've seen the geese and the dyeucks crossin there hunders o times, and surely yer horse his langer legs nor them.'

THEN THERE was the time Jamie was staying at another house and the proprietor and his factor were nearby, discussing a poor crop.

'I've tried many things,' said the factor, 'but nothing seems to grow.'

The man of business, with scant knowledge of farming, mused for a time and was about to give his considered opinion when Jamie interjected, counting factors well down his list of useful articles.

'I cwid tell ye fit wid thrive in't. Plunt it wi factors. They thrive onywye.'

JAMIE, OF course, got his by-name of The Laird o Udny's Fool when he met one of the laird's titled friends in the grounds of the castle.

'Who are you?' asked the gentleman with a superior air.

'I'm the Laird o Udny's feel,' said Jamie. 'Fa's feel are ee?'

REUBEN RAE was a character well known around Kintore in the 1920s, and there was nothing he liked better than to get a lot of young lads round about him so he could boast of all his achievements. The lads were in awe of him, swearing that he was surely in league with the devil.

One of Reuben's tales was of the time a Kintore farmer sent for him as the farm was over-run with rabbits. The farmer met the newly employed trapper a few days later and asked how he was getting on.

'Weel,' Reuben replied, 'last nicht I set thirty-sax snares, and this mornin I hid thirty-sax rubbits and twa wytin ti get in.'

ANOTHER KINTORE worthy was Jamie Will. One day, the young lads had congregated round the fountain when Jamie came past aboard his rather ancient wreck of a bicycle. It was rumoured that he was courting a lass at Balmoral and was en route.

One of the lads suggested: 'It'll tak ye a gey file on that bike, Jamie.'

'Na na,' replied Jamie, sailing past, 'this is ma Sunday bike. Nineteen gears, and fin I get into tap gear, ilky crunk's a quarter o a mile.'

WILLIE LOW, of Glassel, was a well-known dealer, and plenty of stories are attributed to him. Willie had sold a heifer to a neighbouring farmer for £440. Unfortunately, the heifer died a week later, so back came the purchaser to complain and seek recompense.

'Man, Wullie, this is nae damnt eese,' stormed the farmer.

'Fit's adee?' said Willie.

'The heifer's dee't.'

'Man,' said Willie. 'It nivver did that fin I hid it.'

THE INTERNATIONALLY known firm of R.B. Farquhar Ltd was founded by Rab Farquhar, of Rhynie, who started out his business life selling firewood round doors. He never lost the common touch as he became a millionaire, flying the globe to do oil-industry deals. To his immense credit, neither did he lose his strong North-east accent and ways.

Retired banker Edwin Reid had introduced Rab to a British government minister after the minister had made an important speech at the Whitehall Hotel, Houston, Texas.

'Pleased to meet you Mr Farkwar,' said the minister, 'and what do you do for a living?'

Rab didn't like being referred to as Farkwar, but he replied: 'Oh, I jist mak things beginnin wi S.'

'Things beginning with S?' said the minister. 'What sort of things beginning with S?'

'Oh,' said Rab, 'sheds, chalets and shitehooses.'

ON ANOTHER visit to Houston, Edwin took Rab up a downtown skyscraper to view the big city and Mr F. was duly impressed. On their way out, the commissionaire said to the pair of them: 'Y'all have a good weekend, hear?'

Rab turned to Edwin and remarked: 'It was affa nice o that chiel ti say that we maun hae a nice wikkenn,' so Edwin suggested that when Rab got home he should stand at the gates of his factory and greet all his workers with: 'Have a pleasant weekend.'

'Na, na, na,' said Rab. 'I couldna dee that. They wid say that Farquhar's aff his heid.'

RAB BUILT and owned a chalet holiday complex at Callander, and would make frequent runs down in his Rolls-Royce to check up on standards and to be sure that everything was in order. One day when he arrived, he found that the handyman was missing, so he went into the shed, put on a pair of dungarees and started up the mower.

The sound of the mower brought out the slumbering holidaymakers, who were delighted to see a member of staff so that they could bring to his attention whatever little problems they had encountered, from blown light bulbs to new supplies of toilet paper.

Rab delighted in finishing this tale with: 'Ye ken this. I workit real hard aa day and finished up wi a fiver in tips. Then I went back intil the shed, took aff ma dungars, went roon the back, climmed in ower the Rolls-Royce, and I wis jist drivin oot fan a twa-three o them saw me.

'So I wound doon the windae, gied them a wave and I said: "That's me awa hame, than."

'And I could see them starin at me, and then at the car, so I jist said: "Aye, I've an affa good boss."'

. . . and from *Anither Dash o Doric*

HARRY SIM was one of the most colourful councillors in Aberdeenshire local government, and is sadly missed.

Once, he was a Grampian Regional Council delegate to the Offshore Technology Council in Houston, Texas, where anyone who is anyone in the global oil industry has to make an appearance.

As we all know, where high-spending businesspeople gather, working girls are never far behind, and the OTC attracts 'friendly' women from throughout the southern states.

So it was that George Durward, now of Aberdeen, and Harry found themselves sharing a lift in their Houston hotel with a long-limbed ebony beauty, obviously heading off for an evening's commerce.

Presently, her gaze lighted on Harry. She smiled, leaned across to him and suggested that he might be looking for company for the night.

A devoted family man, Harry was outraged. 'Lassie,' he said, pulling himself up to his full five feet, 'awa and dip yer erse in ice cubes.'

THE LEGENDARY Harry Gordon was a national celebrity for his variety shows, comedy sketches and recordings in the Thirties, Forties and Fifties but, outgoing as he was professionally, he liked to keep his private life to himself and was not keen on accepting too many invitations to dinners or parties.

Habitually, when sent an invitation to some function or another, he would reply very courteously:

'Thank you very much for your kind invitation to dinner on Friday next but, unfortunately, I must decline as I cannot be sure that I will be hungry that night.'

THE BUS station at Ballater was in its usual sleepy state one morning in the late 1950s, when Erchie (not his real name; we'll spare him) reported for duty, clocking in at eight, ready to take the wifies in to The Toon on a Saturday-morning shopping spree.

Erchie hadn't many bad habits but, for relaxation, a rug o the pipe stappit wi bogie roll was the very dab.

Inspectors from Bluebird buses (or was it Strachan's at that time?) had the nasty habit of turning up when least expected, and this eagle-eyed official spotted our faithful driver walking into the garage close by the diesel tanks and the No Smoking sign, pipe puffing away like a steam mill.

The inspector followed him in, and here's how a colleague got the first-hand report from our Erchie.

'The peakit-bonnetit mannie challenged me an tellt me I wid be reportit for smokin on duty. Man, I took es cuttie fae ma pooch and I said: "Na, faith ye. Ere's ma pipe and check for yersel. It's steen caul." '

The inspector, although far from impressed, had to admit defeat.

Erchie continued his account: 'Losh, I cwidna get the mannie awa quick eneuch, for the ither pipe wis reid hett and burnin a hole in ma pooch.'

THE LATE Sir Maitland Mackie used to tell a story – he had many – of his farming days at Westerton, Rothienorman.

One of his favourites told of a farmer in earlier days who was always trying to be modern. The usual manure at that time was mixed on the floor of the sheds and then put on to the field. However, the farmer would try the latest on the market – finely ground compounds which the grieve was quite sure could not possibly be any good.

Reluctantly, the grieve had to carry out the boss's wishes and put the men to the work; a happer each, side by side, throwing the stuff out.

Just before lowsin time, the orraman came with the news that there was not sufficient manure to finish out the last wee bit.

The grieve replied: 'Gawa back and tell them ti wug their airms. It'll mak nae bliddy difference.'

GEORGE CLARK, the noted heavy-events athlete on the games scene, took over a hotel at Bonar Bridge and, of course, put out an invitation to his bosom – or boozin – pals to come up North sometime and see his new place.

Three lads, indeed, made the journey once George had settled in, and arrived just on the stroke of 11 – opening time.

After pleasantries had been swapped, the first of the trio said: 'OK, George, we'll hae three drams.'

George reached for the optic and turned back to his pals.

'And which o you three buggers is nae drinkin?'

FOR YEARS, Jimmy Hepburn was manager of the George Walker & Sons fish-selling office at Mallaig, taking over from his father who left Gamrie to start selling for his East Coast firm.

Jimmy didn't suffer fools gladly and it was seldom that anyone got the better of him. A difficult skipper from the East making a rare trip into Mallaig with his catch was not at all happy with the price he was getting, nor the service, and swore that never again would he sell any catch through Jimmy.

'Weel, ma freen,' said Jimmy, his patience at breaking point. 'I'm fifty-four year aul noo and for fifty-three o them I never kent ye existit. I got on gran athoot ye and I'm sure I'll continue that wye even if I nivver see ye again.'

WILLIE GRAY, the Bard o Briggies, summed up a fellow-Donside countryman rather well with the remark:

'Dammit, he's that lazy he cwidna even be bathert ti shak fin he wis caul.'

WILLIE (not our bard we hasten to add) was a gentle soul who lived by himself at Cullerlie and was the orraman at neighbouring farms. He led a rather spartan existence and his intelligence would have been classed as below average.

Coming to autumn, he would go through his annual ritual of storing the fuel for the fire. Peats and sticks would be taken in to his bothy and built up alongside a wall. Paper would be strewn on the floor and the fire lit with the assistance of a suppie paraffin.

One year, the inevitable happened and a massive fire made poor Willie homeless. He was such a lovable character that in no time the neighbours had clubbed together to get him a caravan to be sited on the shell of the bothy because he couldn't bear to leave the area.

The following autumn, Willie began the same ritual of storing his peats and lighting his fires and, sadly, lightning does strike in the same place twice. Once again, his home was destroyed in a raging blaze. With the walls of the caravan being flimsy, this one was much quicker than the first.

The fire brigade from Alford attended as they had done on the previous occasion, and fireman Jock Milne, one of the most notorious characters in the Howe of Alford, said:

'Michty Willie, mind me ti gie ye a calendar at Christmas. Ye're wir best customer.'

SADLY, IT was decided that Willie had to uproot, and he found a home in a complex at Oldmeldrum for elderly people. It didn't take him long to settle, however, as two friends discovered when they went to visit him. Willie was proud to show them round 'his place'.

'Es is ma bedroom. Es is far I sleeps. Es is the lounge far we aa watch the tee vee and play cairds.'

Then, opening the bathroom door, he said: 'And es is the dipper. They've hid me in twice.'

CHARLIE ROSS, the forester, and Harry, the souter o Dunecht, were great pals – Harry being the father of one of your co-authors.

They had been in Garlogie Bar, a mere four miles from base, when the souter expressed a wee bit of anxiety that 'it wis time they were takkin the road'.

'Michty souter,' said the forester, 'time for anither een.'

That one for the road was doubled and trebled, with the souter getting more and more agitated.

'Lord, Harry,' said our happy forester. 'Tak my advice. If ye're five meenits late, ye get a bugger o a row. If ye're five days late, she's damnt gled tae see ye.'

THE LATE John Mearns, that doyen of couthy country humour, was compèring a concert at the Burns Club in Aberdeen. Among the soloists was his wife, Alice. She was requested to sing the 'Back o Bennachie', and unaccompanied, since no piano was available.

Unfortunately, she started a key higher than was comfortable for her, but she struggled on to the usual applause.

Coming back on stage, John said: 'Weel, Alice, Bennachie's nae affa hich, bit it's been some hich for you the nicht.'

IN THE Thirties and Forties, Nath the Donkey was a well-known figure in the Buckie area as he plied his trade, selling vegetables and bartering household items for rags. This was all done from a small cart drawn by a donkey.

On one of his weekly visits to Findochty, the local worthy had bought her veggies and returned indoors only to hear Nath shouting loud abuse at his donkey. Back out she came and said: 'Guid be here, Nath. Fit's aa the tidee?'

'It's ma donkey,' the merchant replied. 'It winna shift an inch and I've tried aathing.'

Our redoubtable lady had the answer.

'Weel, Nath, jist ee peel een o yer ingins and stick half o't up the donkey's doup.'

This he did and the donkey shot off at great haste leaving Nath on the pavement starin at the vanishin cart.

'Oh me, oh me. Fit wye wull I get him back noo?'

'Weel,' said the wife. 'Try shovin the ither half up yer ain doup.'

IAN MIDDLETON told of Kirsty, a redoubtable figure in Buckie in the Sixties, who was becoming decidedly peeved that a nosy male neighbour was for ever glowering into her window every time he passed her house.

One July, in the middle of a great day of heat, Kirsty had opened her window to let in a blaa of fresh air. The nosy mannie took this as an invitation to have a longer glower, and Kirsty's patience finally snapped.

Throwing up her skirt, she stuck her rump to the window and shouted: 'Can ye nae read sma print?!'

DOD MURRAY was a well-loved Buckie skipper with a great wit and tolerance, but he was fed up with one of his crew, who was telling his mates constantly that his wife was 'an angel'.

'That's gran,' said Dod. 'I'm rale pleased for ye. Mine's aye livin.'

The Toon

*The friendly rivalry between city and country, Teuchter
and Toonser, is at its best in their sense of humour. Here
are a few examples of golden wit from the Silver City.*

SHORTLY AFTER Aberdeen set fire to its trams in that
disgraceful ceremony at the beach in the early 1960s,
the city's public transport became all-bus. Some of the
less-swack Aberdonians complained that some of the bus
platforms were too high for them to negotiate and, for
several months, conductors and clippies had to bear the
brunt of the moaning.

One afternoon, outside Watt and Grant's store in Union
Street, a particularly fat woman was struggling to haul
herself aboard.

'Come awa, mither,' said the conductor, offering her a
helping haul. 'I doot ye need some yeast. It'll mak ye rise
better.'

'Tak some yersel,' puffed the woman. 'It'll mak ye
better-bred.'

A FIRM of Aberdeen electricians had been rewiring a
council scheme on the outskirts of the city in the early
1960s and one of the sparkies, a lad so good-looking that
he should have been a model or in films, had taken the
fancy of a bored housewife. To the amusement of his mates,
he would often repair for an hour in the afternoon to the
lady's boudoir and return looking flushed, but relaxed.

One evening, back at the yard, one of the foremen
shouted across to him:

'Aye, Jack, ye'll be awa back til yer new girlfriend's
the nicht?'

'Na,' he called back. 'Ye dinna think I dee that kinna
thing in ma ain time, d'ye?'

ONE CHRISTMAS in the early 1950s, the famed Aberdeen

department store of Esslemont and Macintosh offered an embroidery service for silk stockings. Most women who took up the offer chose to have their initials or monogram embroidered around the stocking tops.

An authoritative source reports that one sparky young woman came in and asked if there would be enough room to embroider:

If you can read this, you are too close

She was being attended by two assistants, a senior man and a middle-aged woman. The man, professional to the last, didn't turn a hair and inquired simply: 'Block letters or script, madam?'

His colleague added drily: 'Or Braille, maybe?'

EVERY LORD Provost of Aberdeen dreams of the affection and regard offered to the most celebrated of his predecessors, Tommy Mitchell, who was Lord Provost during World War II. The most celebrated story, perhaps apocryphal, but with a ring of truth, tells of Lord Provost Mitchell at the Joint Station meeting the Royal Train as King George and Queen Elizabeth arrived with Princesses Elizabeth and Margaret for a short and well-earned break at Balmoral.

As the party turned to make their way from the platform, Tommy drew the Queen to one side and inquired: 'Is ony o the twa quinies needin the lavvie?'

ONE OF Aberdeen's most notorious post-war prostitutes was spending one of her many nights in the Lodge Walk cells when, on the Sunday morning, a great racket got up as she banged a tin cup repeatedly against the cell door. During the night, her period had arrived and she bawled at the top of her voice: 'I want Tampax! I want Tampax!'

The duty officer rushed up and told her to be quiet. 'Ye'll tak porridge like abody else.'

WHEN PROVOST Mitchell was well into his tenure, it is said that he became very concerned about the drinking of one of the city councillors, who tippled so heavily that he could become a great embarrassment on ceremonial occasions, or when dignitaries were paying official visits to Aberdeen.

At one Town House function, when a party of French politicians was being honoured with an official dinner, the councillor approached Tommy during the cocktails, before the dinner had even begun, and said: 'Well, Lord Provost, I must be saying goodbye and thank you.'

Much relieved, Tommy made a pretence of being disappointed and said: 'Must ye be awa this early?'

Then he paused. 'Or are ye bidin and jist sayin cheerio as lang ye can still recognise me?'

A RETIRED civil servant reports taking his car to one of Aberdeen's newest dealers where he sat beside a huge internal window to watch the goings-on in the service bay.

While he waited, he was struck by the work of one particular mechanic, who seemed to be more painstaking than the others.

The mechanic changed the oil without spilling a drop. He lifted the bonnet and placed the prop with the greatest care, checked the water level, then lowered the bonnet gently and clicked it shut.

Then he cleaned the windscreen and, after washing his hands, drove the car carefully out of the service-bay door and into the car park.

Just then, the service manager came to tell the customer that his car was ready.

'Well,' said the customer, 'I can't help admiring the quality of that man's work. I just hope he was the man who worked on my car. I couldn't believe how careful he was with that one.'

'Aye,' said the service manager. 'That wid be because it's his.'

A RETIRED farmer had moved into one of the leafier parts of Aberdeen's West End to stay with his son and daughter-in-law and was in the habit of taking an afternoon constitutional. Not many doors up the street, a young couple had moved in and word had got around that the wife was from Stuttgart, which was enough for the old boy to go for an investigative stroll.

One afternoon, he spotted the young wife working in her front garden and he set off down his garden path, walking slowly. Once out along the pavement, he stopped beside her and leaned on her garden fence.

'Aye-aye,' he said.

She looked up into the sun, smiled and said hello.

'Ye're German,' he said.

'Well, yes, I am,' she said, and a silence hung heavily between them for a few moments.

'The Germans drappit a bomb on this street durin the war.'

She wasn't quite sure what she was supposed to say, so she waited. And he waited.

Then he stepped back and, just as he was about to leave, said: 'Dinna fash yersel. It didna ging aff.'

AN ABERDEEN taxi-driver, a Mr Duncan, was sitting in the Back Wynd taxi rank in the wee sma oors when a group of four young men, almost unconscious with drink, were led down the street by two of their slightly more sober friends.

The men collapsed into the taxi and one of the half-sober chums leaned into the window and gave Mr Duncan a list of addresses and pointed out which drunk was to be deposited at which address.

Mr Duncan drove off but, for a bit of fun, drove round the block and back in time to see the two half-sober men still standing there, chatting to two young women. He wound down the window and called the two lads over.

'Ye hinna forgotten the addresses?' said one.

'No,' said Mr Duncan, 'could ye sort oot yer pals again? I hit a bump.'

A TORY candidate between the wars was fighting the unwinnable seat of Aberdeen North and was addressing a largely hostile meeting. One Fittie woman was particularly disparaging about Conservative policy and the party's promises for the area, and was not shy of heckling him to tell him so.

The candidate took it for so long, but eventually snapped. 'Madam,' he said, fixing her with a glare from the platform, 'you have enough brass in your neck to make a kettle.'

'Aye,' shouted the fisherwife, 'and you've enough watter in yer heid ti fill it.'

DURING THE war, Mrs Chris Clark had a job in a workmen's café with another assistant, Lizzie, who was allowed to take her four-year-old daughter, Betty, in for meals.

One day, Mrs Clark heard Betty being reprimanded for her table manners.

'Noo, Betty,' said Lizzie. 'Foo often div I hae ti tell ye? Ye dinna pit yer moo doon til the sasser fin ye drink yer tea.'

'No?'

'No. Ye lift the sasser up til yer moo.'

IN THE late 1950s, or perhaps early 1960s, the then Lord Aberdeen ventured to the telephone office in Aberdeen to pay his account. The male clerk behind the counter accepted the cheque, which had been signed 'Aberdeen'. Unfortunately, he did not recognise Lord Aberdeen and pushed the cheque back towards him, saying:

'Aye, aye, aye, we ken this is Aiberdeen. Now sign yer name.'

BILL SIVEWRIGHT and Ernie Laing were well into their

eighties and were sitting in the funeral cortege in the car behind the hearse as it made its way towards the new Aberdeen Crematorium at Hazlehead.

Bill turned to Ernie and said nostalgically: 'Ernie, div ye mind fan we were young? We used to waak ahin the funeral procession. Then a puckle years efter that, we'd be in een o the back cars. Now here we are in the car next til the hearse.'

'Aye,' said Ernie. 'We're weerin closer.'

TOMMY TOSH, now deceased, used to tell of watching the world go by at a street corner in Middlefield one day when he saw a blind man approaching, led by his guide dog. At the street corner, just a few feet from Tommy, the dog lifted its leg and urinated all over his master's trousers. The blind man felt in his pocket and took out a biscuit, which he gave to the dog.

'Aye,' said Tommy, 'I've seen some real kind things, bit that's real touchin. Yer dog peed a ower ye and ye still gied it a biscuit.'

'Kind be damnt,' said the blind man. 'Now that I ken far his moo is, I can kick his erse.'

ADAM DUGUID, of Hazlehead, Aberdeen, reports attending a concert at the Tivoli Theatre, Aberdeen, in the early 1960s. It was a variety show, but he specifically wanted to see one of his great heroes, trombonist George Chisholm.

Adam was enjoying another masterly performance by George, when he heard the young woman sitting in front of him lean closer to the lad next to her and say: 'Is he really swallyin that thing?'

WHEN JACK Robertson, of Middlefield, ran out of cigarettes at the Fish Market one day, he asked a fellow-porter for a match, thinking that that would spur the man into offering a cigarette, too.

Jack took the offered match, patted his overalls and said: 'Dash it, I doot I've left ma fags at hame, as weel.'

The colleague reached over. 'In that case,' he said. 'Ye winna be needin the match.'

. . . and from *Anither Dash o Doric*

FRANK TAYLOR was a post-war delivery driver for Paterson's, the wholesale chemist's in Aberdeen, and was a weel-kent figure around the city, with his faithful horse, laden cart and Trixie the dog.

One day, Mitchell Ross, owner of the firm, decided that the march of progress was inevitable and informed Frank that the horse would have to be retired and that he would be issued with a brand-new Commer truck.

Frank was none too happy, but agreed to the change.

After several weeks without his beloved horse, a city chemist asked Jack how he was getting on with the Commer.

'Ach,' said Frank. 'The horse kept awa fae the traffic, but this bugger gyangs stracht for it.'

THE TALES of the country-bred waitress at the old Gloucester Hotel, which we featured in *A Dash o Doric*, seemed to take a trick, especially with those readers who remembered the doughty lady only too well. Bette Fraser, now living in Dunfermline, remembers being invited out by a boyfriend in the late 1950s and finishing with dinner at the Gloucester.

'I can't be certain that your waitress and mine were the same,' she wrote, 'but her tongue was razor-sharp and she was very entertaining with it. To be perfectly honest, I had grown tired of my young man, for he was a wee bit full of himself and a bit showy-offy, and it was time he was taken down a peg.

'The waitress came to ask if we would like a drink before our meal, and my lad puffed out his chest and said: "Yes, I think I will have a G and T." Then he laughed in her face and said: "That's a gin and tonic."

'"Is that so?" she said. "And wid ye like ice and lemon? That's frozen watter and sliced fruit."'

THE SAME doughty waitress is supposed to have been stopped by a breakfast guest who wanted to complain that his egg was off.

She glared at him and said: 'I only biled it. I didna lay it.'

AND STILL in full flight, she is supposed to have served a cup of coffee to a QC who was having a break from court. Unfortunately, he had not been given a teaspoon.

He made a grave error in trying sarcasm. 'Waitress,' he said, 'this coffee is a little too hot to stir with my fingers, isn't it?'

'Ach weel,' she said, sailing past, 'wait a twa-three minties and try again.'

SOME YEARS ago, when Brazil were playing Scotland in a friendly international at Hampden, there was a sizeable exodus from the North-east eager to lend support to the boys in blue.

Two of Torry's finest found themselves outside the national stadium and spotted a dusky-skinned gentleman, obviously from South America, looking a little lost. They decided to see if they could help.

'Aye-aye,' said one. 'Ye're lookin lost. Far are ye fae?'

The Brazilian looked mystified.

'Where – are – you – fae?' said the other Aberdonian.

The foreigner brightened. 'Ah. I am from Rio de Janeiro.'

'Rio de Janeiro?' said one of the Torry loons. 'Michty, fit time did ye leave the hoose?'

EILEEN DUNN started work at the Watt & Grant store in Union Street shortly before the war and recalls two country wifies leaving after having spent fully three hours raking through frocks and trying on this, that and the other.

Eventually, they left having purchased nothing, but Eileen heard one say to the other as they headed for the door:

'I really likit that green een, Jessie.'

'Ay,' said Jessie, 'it wid hiv fittit ye if ye could hiv got it on.'

TOWARDS THE end of her career, Eileen worked among lingerie and recalls a very shy and embarrassed young man turning up and surveying the goods on sale. Eileen debated whether or not he might want help or if he might find that offputting.

Eventually, she approached him and asked quietly if he needed assistance.

'Ay, w-well,' he stammered. 'I w-wis lookin for a silk nightie or something.'

'Certainly,' said Eileen. 'What size and what colour and I'll show you a few styles?'

A little happier with himself, the young chap looked through the items which Eileen had spread out on the counter and, as he surveyed, he mentioned that it was a birthday present for his wife.

'Oh, lovely,' said Eileen. 'When's her birthday?'

'It's nae her birthday,' he said. 'It's my birthday.'

EILEEN ALSO recalls serving two women who had arrived in the store one Saturday in April. One woman was looking for an outfit for a forthcoming wedding, and her friend was there to give a second opinion.

The customer went through several dresses, each with less success than the one before, until eventually the friend studied the seventh attempt and said: 'Nae really.'

'Nae really?' snapped the customer to her friend. 'Fit div ye mean nae really? Is it the wrang colour? The wrang style? The wrang linth? Fit is't?'

The friend walked forward and patted her chum on the shoulder. 'Pit it this wye, Ina. Ye look lik a bugfae o cats awa ti be droont.'

SHEILA INNES, of Mannofield, Aberdeen, was sitting having lunch in rather a rundown city-centre café one day listening to the old couple at the next table. The woman was chawing happily at her bradie and chips, but the old boy clearly did not rate the cuisine very highly and grumbled all the way through.

Shortly before Sheila was due to go, a plumber's van arrived outside and the plumber and his mate took various hacksaws, blowlamps, hammers and spanners from the back of the van and marched into the shop.

'Ay boys,' said the old grumbler, looking up. 'I see ye've aeten here afore.'

JIMMY MAUCHRIE was a famous old-style barber in George Street until his early death in 1958. The story goes that a bald gentleman turned up for a trim but, before he sat down, he wanted to know how much he would be charged.

When he found out he would be charged the normal price for a trim, he objected strongly.

'Ye're nae tellin me ye're chargin full price for a haircut and me wi sae little hair?'

'I am,' said Jimmy. 'Cuttin yer hair hardly costs onythin. The pricey bit's findin it.'

POSTIE BARRY had just returned to his base at the Head Post Office in Crown Street, Aberdeen, after his first delivery and told his colleague that he had been stung by a wasp on his rounds.

'Far aboot?' inquired John.

'Osborne Place.'

DOLLY AND Harry Birnie, of Aberdeen, were on holiday

in London. On the last day, they were looking for those obligatory last-minute take-home presents.

They couldn't forget their dear friend Alfie back home in the Granite City, an inveterate smoker, so that was why they came to enter a very posh tobacconist's shop in the Bond Street area.

They were shown a wide selection of pipes, but were recommended one meerschaum in particular which was very, very expensive.

Dolly examined the pipe, put it back down on the counter and said to the pukka gentleman at the other side.

'Ach, no. At's ower muckle. He'll jist let it fa, trump on't an brakk it.'

They departed the shop leaving behind a totally bewildered assistant.

A MAJOR fish-processing firm in Poynernook Road, Aberdeen, had just installed the latest in machinery, with filleting and packing lines instead of the conventional tables.

The filleters on the line, upwards of fifty perhaps, were mostly women and it was a new and daunting experience for the young male management to run the gauntlet of the tongues of the fishwives.

In fact, it became too much; the wifies won with their wit every time, so the production manager and his sidekick decided on safety in numbers.

From thenceforth, they would inspect the work in pairs, most distinctive in their white coats, wellies and starched hats.

With such a close relationship, it didn't take the filleting quines long to chorus:

'Here they are again – semmit and draa'ers.'

The Papers

The Press and Journal, Evening Express *and a whole raft of weeklies from Forres to Montrose have recorded thousands of funny Doric stories in their time. Often, the funniest are those which befall the reporters and writers.*

WHEN A writer from the *Press and Journal* was dispatched to tell first-year pupils at Turriff Academy about life as a journalist, the class sat dutifully through his talk as he explained about training, use of English, knowledge of law, an ability to get on with people, persistence and long hours.

When he finished, he invited questions, but, as in many North-east schools, the class was too shy. Despite repeated requests, no one could be persuaded to ask anything.

The *P&J*'s man decided to go into a little of the history of the paper, for it's not commonly understood that the *Press and Journal* is the third-oldest English-language newspaper in the world. He explained that it had been established in December, 1747, and had published its first copy in January, 1748. It had been founded by a man called James Chalmers.

At that, a ripple of laughter started in one of the back corners and many others in the class turned to see what was happening.

'What is it?' asked the *P&J* man. 'Have I said something funny?'

'No,' said one of the class pointing at a fellow-pupil, 'but his name's Chalmers.'

'Oh, well,' said the *P&J* man. 'It could even be that the P. *and J*. was founded by one of your ancestors.'

'Nuh,' said the pupil in question.

'Oh, but how can you be so sure?'

'Hinna got ony ancestors.'

AT ANOTHER schools talk, the same writer invited questions and, again, no one could be persuaded out of their shyness. 'Come on, now,' he said. 'Surely someone has a question.'

Eventually, a shy little thing in the front row put up her hand.

'Yes,' he said. 'What would you like to know?'

'Far did ye get yer sheen?' she asked in a very small voice.

'My shoes?' he said, trying not to look surprised. 'Well, I think it was a shop at Inverurie. Why? Do you like them?'

She looked at the shoes and then looked up at him.

'Nae really.'

THE SAME writer was dispatched to a Donside school to talk to pupils there and found them in the middle of a maths lesson. Being a forward-looking school, the maths lesson took a practical form. The teacher had written out a cake recipe and had asked the pupils to work out a proportion sum by converting a recipe for ten servings to a recipe for sixteen.

To test their skills, the cake had been baked. As guest for the afternoon, the *Press and Journal*'s man was invited to cut the cake and sample the first slice, so he pointedly made a fuss of how tasty it was.

Then teacher invited all the others in the class to have a piece, and all clamoured forward. All apart from one boy, who stood at the back, not eating.

'What's the matter?' said the *Press and Journal*'s man, 'are you not having a slice of your delicious cake?'

'Na,' he said. 'I ken fit I put in it.'

THE SAME man reports attending a small WRI in the middle of Aberdeenshire, again for the purposes of giving a talk. After speaking for forty minutes, he was invited to take tea with the committee. Somehow – he is not entirely sure – a strip of raffle tickets appeared at his side and, worried in case someone had mislaid them, he drew the president to one side and pointed them out.

'Na, na,' she said. 'That's your strippie, that. We aye buy a strippie for wir guest spikker.'

He thanked her kindly and sat back, waiting for the numbers to be drawn.

Then she stepped back towards him and said: 'And we hope ye dinna win.'

ONE MORNING in the mid-1980s, all the radio-network wavelengths in North-east Scotland changed to try to tidy up the airwaves. Realising that great confusion was likely as the region tried to retune thousands of radios, the BBC and the IBA had been plugging the changeover for weeks and, on the Monday morning, the *Press and Journal* published a big notice explaining as much.

Shortly after 12.30pm, the features editor of the paper took a call from a very frail, elderly voice. 'I canna find Robbie Shepherd,' she wailed.

'Well, all the radio stations changed today,' said the features editor. 'Have you retuned your radio?'

'Oh, I did hear something aboot that, bit I dinna ken nithing aboot radios,' she said.

'All right. All right,' said the features editor. 'Do you have your paper in front of you?'

'Aye.'

'Is it open at the TV page?'

'Aye.'

'And do you see where it says Radio Aberdeen?'

'Aye.'

'Do you see a three-figure number next to Radio Aberdeen?'

'Aye.'

'Well, if you turn the dial on your radio to where it says that three-figure number, you'll get Robbie Shepherd.'

'Bit I dinna think it says onything on ma radio.'

'Does it not say anything on the top of your radio?'

'Wait a mintie.' And he heard the sound of footsteps walking slowly over to the other side of the room. A few seconds later, they returned and the phone was lifted.

'No, it disna say nithing on the top o ma radio.'

'Does it not say anything on the front of your radio, then?'

'Jist a mintie.' And the footsteps went off again.

Back they came. 'No, it disna say nithing on the front o ma radio, eether.'

'Well, what about the back of your radio?'

'Jist a mintie.' Off she went and back she came, this time with a note of triumph in her voice.

'Yes, it dis say something on the back o ma radio.'

'What does it say?'

'Made in Taiwan.'

THE FAREWELL gift is a tradition in offices up and down the land but journalism, in which the pool of available professional talent is remarkably small, frequently sees careers move in spirals, with some hacks returning to the scenes of their cub days before moving onward and upward yet again.

The *Press and Journal* was home to one particularly nomadic chap, who stayed for a few months, moved on, and returned every couple of years to stay for several more months, before moving on, and so on.

Each time, a whipround provided him with a handsome farewell gift until, on the fourth occasion, the large buff envelope presented to a particularly gruff sports writer brought a curt wave-away and: 'Season ticket.'

JIMMY GRANT was one of the most celebrated journalists the North-east has ever produced, and was editor of the *Press and Journal* until he retired in 1975. Once invited to a garden party at Holyroodhouse, he accepted, but was determined not to be outdone by the great and the good who, he knew, would be sporting chestfuls of medals.

On the day in question, Jimmy turned up wearing a large silvery medallion which impressed all who saw him. It caused great interest, and when one acquaintance bumped into him and commented on it, he winked and held it out for study.

It had belonged to his mother, as the legend explained:

Turriff Show. Best Butter. 1933.

ONE YOUNG journalist once asked Jimmy Grant why so many people bought the *Press and Journal* in small country villages and towns when, one would expect, everyone knew everyone else's business, anyway.

'Aye,' said Jimmy, 'they do. But they read the paper to see fa's been caught at it.'

A FORMER *Evening Express* reporter remembers going to a tenement in Torry to interview a former fisherman who had reached the ripe old age of 100. As is customary, he asked the birthday boy to what he attributed his old age.

The man thought for quite a while and said: 'Faith in the Lord. Get up early. Dinna sweir. Dinna drink. And dinna smoke.'

The reporter duly noted all this down, saying: 'Well, that's marvellous. Mind you, I had an uncle at Elgin and that was exactly the way he lived and he died at eighty-two. How do you account for that?'

'Aweel,' grinned the fisherman. 'He surely didna keep it up lang enough.'

ONE OF the facts of newspaper life is that everyone will disagree with something. Some say that a newspaper that doesn't annoy a good few of its readers every morning isn't doing its job properly. These days, provided that a complaint is genuine and proven, any newspaper will do its best to correct any error for which it is responsible.

The complaints which are merely differences of opinion are another matter. In these days of customer care, readers whose complaints are merely prejudices will be let down as gently as possible and told why a 'correction' is not possible – because nothing was wrong in the first place.

It was not always so gentle. One editor of a daily paper happened to be passing the newsdesk phone ringing one evening and picked it up. He was treated to a tirade of abuse for the coverage of what had seemed a perfectly innocent report of a minor political meeting. The caller felt that his party had not been given due credit and space. The editor, whose job it is to decide who gets what coverage, listened stoically while an aspiring politician lectured him on how to do his job.

He tried several times to interrupt and explain the paper's policy, but the party man was determined to have his say. Eventually, the editor decided to wait for the flow of invective to falter, then said: 'Excuse me, do you know who you're talking to?'

'I do not.'

'Then bugger off.'

A *PRESS and Journal* man was dispatched to a schools careers evening at Inverurie Academy and was duly manning the stand when an extremely reluctant and gangly youth was propelled towards him by a portly gent with the ruddy face and gnarled hands of a man of the soil. The *Press and Journal* man took them for farmer father and son.

He went through a five-minute explanation of the demands of the job, the qualifications needed and how competitive it was even to get a place on a training programme, let alone a job. Then he asked if the boy had any questions.

'Go on, Gordon,' said the farmer. 'The blokie's askin if ye've a question. Speir awa.'

Gordon did not look up, but mumbled a good North-east

question: 'Fit's the siller like?' The *Press and Journal*
man explained the salary scales and merit awards, trainee
indentures and senior-journalist rates.

'And foo muckle div you mak?' asked Gordon.

The *Press and Journal* man gave his stock answer: 'Well,'
he said. 'More than a pittance, but not quite as much as a
fortune.'

This time, the father leaned forward, with a farmer's
gleam in his eye:

'And foo muckle's that exactly?'

THEY SAY in the Classified Advertising department of
Aberdeen Journals that during a sales promotion offering
seven words for £2, a Buchan family phoned up to place a
death notice and suggested as wording:

'John Reid. Bogheid. Deid.'

'Well, yes,' said the tele-ad girl, 'but that's only four
words and you can have seven for your two pounds.'

'We'll phone ye back,' said the family.

Five minutes later, the phone rang again.

'Right, we've sortit it oot. We'll say:

'John Reid. Bogheid. Deid. Volvo for sale.'

. . . and from *Anither Dash o Doric*

DURING CAMPAIGNING for the 1955 General Election,
it was the practice for candidates to tour constituencies
making up to three speeches a night at various rural halls.
In the days before TV, a good turnout was guaranteed, and
so it was at a hall up one Kincardine glen.

Jimmy Lees, then an Aberdeen Journals reporter, reckons
that the audience topped 100, made up mostly of farmers,
farm-workers and wives, all waiting to hear what the
candidate would have to say.

But the candidate was late and the minutes ticked away – ten, twenty, then half an hour.

With the audience becoming restless, the MC, a local farmer himself, tried to steady the assembly by calling from the stage: 'A'richt, a'richt, ladies and gentlemen, as ye can see, the candidate's a bittie late, bit I've nae doot he'll be here afore lang. Hooivver, we'll fill in the time wi a discussion, I think. Now, fit will we discuss? His onybody got a suggestion?'

There was silence in the hall.

'Naebody ata?' said the MC. 'A'richt, I'll pick a subject masel.'

He thought for a moment, then brightened.

'I ken,' he said. 'Seein that this rural depopulation's worryin abody, we'll hae a discussion on that. Now, we ken it's a problem. We'll seen hae nae fowk left up the glens. So, tell me noo, foo wid ye stop rural depopulation?'

'Nae bother,' came a shout from the back. 'Lat louse yer grieve.'

FROM TIME to time, Radio 1 forsakes its London studios and travels around the country. On one occasion in the late 1980s, the station broadcast its entire live output from Aberdeen and, for a whole morning, from the premises of Aberdeen Journals.

A succession of DJs on the morning in question toured the various departments, broadcasting to the nation from the likes of the press room, the editorial hall and the advertising building.

The broadcast from Advertising fell to Bruno Brookes, who decided that he would like to interview an advertising rep and asked for a suitable nominee, but the young woman who was volunteered seemed not at all happy about broadcasting live to millions across the nation. We'll call her Joanne to spare her blushes.

To try to put her at her ease, Bruno said he would give her a little rehearsal while the two-minute news bulletin was being broadcast. Sure enough, when the news began, he explained to Joanne that he would ask her an easy-enough question about the cost of advertising in regional papers these days, and wasn't it horrendously expensive. 'What will your reply be?' he asked.

Joanne was prompted by her colleagues to point out that, for the money, advertisers were getting unparalleled access to virtually half the adult population of the North of Scotland so that the per-head fee was one of the lowest of any form of advertising. Not only that, but newspaper advertising's track record in shifting goods for sale remained unmatched.

Joanne felt happy with that, but looked anxiously at the microphone in front of her and at the location manager counting down the seconds until the broadcast went live to the nation once more. A light sweat appeared on her brow.

Once the news had finished and the red light had illuminated in front of Bruno Brookes, he began in his customarily bouncy style:

'Welcome back to Aberdeen, where we're broadcasting across the nation from one of Scotland's leading newspaper companies. With me is Joanne, who sells advertising for two of the most successful newspapers in the country. Now, tell me, Joanne, people say to me that it's all very well advertising in newspapers, but it's very expensive. Now, tell me honestly, as the expert you are, the cost is really horrific, isn't it?'

Joanne swallowed hard, began sweating profusely, looked at the mike and said:

'Ay.'

DOUG PRATT, a reporter from the *Press and Journal*, had been sent out to meet a centenarian in a Church of Scotland eventide home in Aberdeen and had been surprised and delighted to find a sparky, elegant and lively woman who looked at least twenty years younger, with hair newly done, a little make-up, new frock and clearly enjoying being the centre of attention.

'Tell me,' said Doug, 'why do you suppose you've been able to live to be a hundred?'

She leaned forward and tapped his knee mischievously.

'The good Lord enjoys lettin me annoy ivry ither bugger in here.'

WHEN 'MAD' Colin Mitchell was campaigning as Tory candidate for West Aberdeenshire in 1970, he attended a lively meeting at Inverurie Town Hall. Mad Mitch was lamenting the fact that unemployment seemed to be increasing under the Labour government and that many more people were on short-term working contracts. He spotted one dejected looking soul in the second row and asked him:

'You, sir. Are you in work?'

The man nodded.

'And what time do you go to work?'

The man removed his bunnet, scratched his head and sighed: 'I'm a fairmer. I dinna ging ti work. Ilky mornin I wakken up, I'm surroundit wi the bliddy stuff.'

THE HIGHLAND Games scene in Grampian area has its climax at the famed Braemar Gathering in the Princess Royal and Duke of Fife Memorial Park. The attendance of members of the Royal Family as they holiday at Balmoral swells the crowd to around 20,000, but it extends the resources of the security forces and puts pressure on the committee who put on the gathering.

Perhaps it's his rustic Deeside upbringing, but organising secretary Bill Meston takes each problem as it comes and one came early one year in the form of a persistent Pressman who was anxious to speak to Bill as secretary, even although his channel of communication should have been the Press tent.

He had already had two abortive sorties into the small

secretary's tent to be told that Bill was out on the field somewhere.

On his third visit he tried again, and there he was face-to-face with Bill, whom he didn't know.

'Is Mr Meston around *now*?' enquired our anxious hack-cum-photographer.

Rather than explain the whole rigmarole of the procedures to be adhered to through the two officials in charge of the Press tent, the reply from Bill was short but effective.

'Losh, he canna be far awa; I've been wi him aa mornin.'

IT'S GOING back a wee bit, but it shows that your authors have the North-east at heart.

It's so long ago that your co-author cannot recall the date when Alastair Robertson wrote a column in the *Evening Express* – Bon-Accord Gossip – and it featured a dilemma facing Robbie.

There had come an invitation for him to compère the Scottish Fiddle Orchestra, conducted by the redoubtable John Mason MBE – at the Royal Albert Hall in London.

Unfortunately, it coincided with Meldrum Sports and our commentator politely refused the London invitation. This prompted Mr Robertson to write:

'Robbie Shepherd forsakes glamour of city lights of London to commentate on egg-and-spoon race at Meldrum.'

SPOTTED IN one weekly paper's report from the small courts:

'*A woman has been charged with growing cannabis at Huntly Sheriff Court.*'

Michty, fit's the law comin til?

THE *Press and Journal* has a network of what are known in the trade as corrs, short for correspondents. These are people in towns, villages and parishes throughout the paper's circulation area – the northern half of Scotland

– who are of good character and who can keep an ear to the ground for likely stories.

Some of the more accomplished are trusted almost as professional reporters and the newsdesk relies on them to do a near-professional job, which is why, in the 1964 election, it was a corr who was assigned to cover the count of one North-east constituency, mainly because the result was judged to be a walkover for the sitting member, and there was not likely to be anything untoward to demand the efforts of a professional newsman.

Unfortunately, as well as taking details of the count, the corr had partaken a little too heavily of the hospitality. Back in Aberdeen, the newsdesk staff were becoming more and more anxious that what should have been a straight-forward phone-in seemed to be getting perilously close to edition time.

Eventually, the corr phoned.

'And the reshult here,' he slurred, '. . . is . . . is . . . and the reshult . . . the reshult . . . the v-v-vohhhhhhte . . . the reshult . . . is . . . is. Michty, I'm an affa mess o drink.'

It was the one time the *Press and Journal* missed an election result on its own doorstep, through no fault of its own.

Aches and Pains

The doctor, one of the honoured North-east triumvirate which includes dominie and minister, is held in great respect in villages and towns throughout the North-east to this day. This privileged position gives a doctor a marvellous perspective for seeing North-east wit at its most unwitting.

THE DOCTOR at Tarland, shortly after World War I, was called to the deathbed of a farmer's wife near Coull. The lady was in great pain and it became clear very quickly that there was little that he could do except make her more comfortable. The farmer, a stocky, unexpressive man, stared solidly from the foot of the bed. Three hours later, the lady breathed her last, the doctor performed the duties necessary and the farmer, quite out of character, broke down in tears and fell to his knees.

Three days after the funeral, the doctor met the farmer in the street at Tarland and said: 'In view of your bereavement, I'm prepared to forget about half my bill.'

'That's rale decent o ye, doctor,' said the farmer. 'And seein as it's yersel, I'll forget aboot the ither half.'

SHORTLY AFTER Aberdeen's spanking new Royal Infirmary was opened in the mid-1930s (largely by public subscription, which gives the lie to the North-east reputation for grip), a workman's bothy caught fire at the eastern end of the site.

Rather than cause a panic in the nearest wards, nursing sisters instructed their staff to draw screens round the beds so that patients need not become overwrought.

One patient who came round after an operation saw the screens and asked: 'Fit wye the screens? Did ye nae expect me ti recover?'

'No,' said the nurse. 'It's nae that. A bothy ootside the windae catched fire and we didna wint ye ti see the flames and think the worst hid happened.'

ONE RETIRED Donside doctor reports a tale from his days as a medical student at Aberdeen University, when a tutor inquired of his tutor group if any of them intended to specialise.

'Oh, yes, indeed,' said one ambitious young Englishman. 'I feel the area that will offer the most interesting medical advances in future will be the diseases of the nose. Most certainly.'

'I see,' said the weary old doctor. 'Just the nose? Not Ear, Nose and Throat?'

'Just the nose,' confirmed the student grandly. 'I feel that the ears and throat are too complicated to be combined with the nose for the purposes of study and treatment.'

'Hmm,' said the old doctor. 'And will you concentrate on any nostril in particular?'

A SMALL boy who was exceptionally keen on fishing had managed to get a hook fouled in his hand and was taken to the doctor to have the hook removed.

The doctor managed the operation reasonably quickly and, as mother and son made towards the door, he noticed that the boy was hanging back. 'Is there something else?' he asked the boy.

'Aye,' said the lad. 'Gies back ma hook.'

DURING THE war, men of a certain age had to go through a medical before being enlisted. The medical panel came across one chap they thought was skiving and decided to try to catch him out.

'What is the time on that clock, Mr D——?' they inquired.

He looked at the clock and replied: 'Couldna tell ye. The only time I ken is fan the twa hans is at the top, and that's dennertime.'

DR DANNY Gordon was a country doctor who practised at Ellon for many years and was held in the highest regard. He used to tell a story, from pre-NHS days, of how he was called out to a confinement and it was to be the arrival of a fifth child to a Mrs MacGregor.

The midwife was waiting anxiously by the front door.

'Fit ail't ye, doctor, and Mrs MacGregor wytin sair for ye?'

Dr Danny made little comment, but went about his own couthy but professional way.

'What kept me?' he used to chuckle many years later. 'I could have said plenty, bit I wis there in time for the call o duty and, to tell ye the truth, I hidna been peyed for the safe arrival o the ither fower.'

AUL RIDDELL was a gamekeeper on a Donside estate just after the war and was persuaded by his wife, after much pressure and nagging, to visit the doctor to see about his shortness of breath and stomach pains. After seventy years of never a day's illness, he knew himself he wasn't any longer in the best of condition. He wasn't able to tramp the hills in pursuit of the grouse, and was beginning to fail in his duties in organising a shoot.

After the usual examination and questions about lifestyle, the doctor got to the truth of the matter. Putting the stethoscope aside, he felt around the gamie's rotund frame and sighed.

'I suggest, Mr Riddell, that you'll have to cut out the drink and the cigarettes.'

Looking up from the couch, the gamie grunted and mused. 'I see. I see. And hiv ye a knife, doctor?'

The doctor, somewhat taken aback, asked why.

'Because if ye're makkin me dee athoot ma drink and ma fags, ye micht as weel cut aff the mannie and get rid o a ma pleesures at the same time.'

IN THE days before the National Health Service, not a million miles from the Cabrach, Dr Scott was called to attend a farmhouse where a young maidservant seemed to be suffering from severe depression.

On arriving, the good doctor tried out the psychology

and experience of a rural practitioner – the techniques these kindly men had in abundance. After a lengthy chat in his best bedside manner, he realised that the kitchie deem had simply taken to bed in the sulks because the farmer had not paid her wages for five or six weeks. It was an early and inspired form of industrial action.

'I'll lie him oot,' she confided. 'He'll pey up afore I tak ma body aff this bed.'

'Noo lassie,' said the soothing tones of the doctor. 'Jist ee lie ower a bittie and I'll get in aside ye. He hisna peyed me, eether.'

THIS ONE comes from a relative of one of your co-authors' families. Aunt Mary was a nurse and on duty in the out-patient's department of Aberdeen Royal Infirmary. An elderly lady, a little confused, was ushered into the ward, told to lie down on the bed and the consultant would be round to visit her shortly.

Along came the man of authority and, with the screens round about the bed, he started the usual pleasantries with a remark on how well she was getting on.

'Now,' he said gently, 'if you would just take down your pants.'

There was no response; not even a flicker of an eyelid from the old lady on the bed.

'I say, please take down your pants.'

Still nothing.

After repeating the request at least twice more, the exasperated consultant was almost shouting when he said: 'Mrs B——, I have a long list of patients in front of me and I really must hurry you up. Will you please take down your knickers?'

The woman on the bed finally stirred.

'Oh, I'm affa sorry, doctor. Are ye spikkin ti me? I thocht ye wis spikkin til the nursie here.'

IT WAS the first time in hospital for old Willie. He had

never had a day's illness in his life but then, without warning, he was felled by a stroke. The first few days in hospital were a blur, but then he recovered sufficiently to play his part in the daily ritual of hospital life.

Wakened at the crack of dawn, as is the wont of nursing staff, he was surprised to find the curtains drawn round about him, with a cheery nurse beside him with a basin full of steaming hot water and all the required toiletries.

'Now, Willie, ye're gettin a bed-bath.'

'Michty, nursie,' said Willie. 'Ye'll nivver get ma erse in that sma basin.'

THE NEXT three are not so much Dashes of Doric, but they are all genuine transcriptions of reports from Aberdeen Royal Infirmary, as told to us by a receptionist.

1. A doctor had dictated on his machine: 'The old man was admitted with severe lower abdominal pain due to constipation.' The resulting transcription read: 'The old man was admitted with severe lower abdominal pain due to constant passion.'

2. A phone call from a GP to the hospital stated that: 'The patient's got a renal colic', which was transcribed into the daily written report for hospital staff as: 'The patient's a real wee comic.'

3. Again from a rural doctor: 'My patient, I'm sure, has a chest complaint, perhaps emphysematous.' This was transcribed on the word-processor as: 'My patient, I'm sure, has a chest complaint, perhaps with his semmit on.'

. . . and from *Anither Dash o Doric*

DR PAT Macdonald, who was in general practice in Aberdeen before retiring to Beaconsfield in the Home Counties of England, told of examining an elderly lady who was very concerned about her health, but who couldn't quite state what she thought was wrong with her or what her symptoms were.

Pat called in the nurse and began the examination, and kept up light-hearted chatter through his questioning, but still could find nothing wrong.

'Well,' he said, sitting back at his desk, 'you'll be pleased to hear that you're as well as can be expected Miss ——. You'll live to be eighty, at least.'

He was horrified when the woman said: 'Bit I am eichty.'

But he said he could have hugged his country-born nurse when, quick as a flash, she stepped in with: 'Weel, so the doctor's richt again.'

OVERHEARD IN the dentist's waiting-room at the Bridge of Don. An elderly lady and her daughter were waiting, and granny, as we'll call her, was to be fitted for a new set of false teeth.

'Weel,' said the daughter, 'I jist hope ye dinna end up lookin lik Esther Rantzen.'

A puzzled look came over granny's face.

'Fa's he?'

IN *A Dash o Doric*, we told the true story of a patient at Aberdeen Royal Infirmary and the aftermath of his operation.

To recap: Willie woke up to find the curtains drawn round about him and a nurse standing there with a basin of hot water, a bar of soap and a towel.

'Now, Willie, ye're gettin a bed-bath.'

'Michty, nursie,' said Willie. 'Ye'll nivver get my erse in that sma basin.'

Now to the other side of the North-easter, and it's in response to that story that we heard from Mrs Sim, of Stoneywood, who had a similar tale but with a different ending.

Sandy was a retiring bachelor in his seventies in similar circumstances to Willie – the curtains, the soap, the basin, and so on.

'Richt Sandy. Ye're gettin on fine noo, so we're gaun tae gie ye a bed-bath.'

But Sandy had never tirred in front of a female before and, after much stuttering and stammering, he said grudgingly:

'Aa richt than, bit jist leave the roch grun ti me.'

A PATIENT at Aberdeen Royal Infirmary was undergoing a stomach operation under a local anaesthetic and was asked by the surgeon if he was feeling all right.

'Aye. I'm aa richt,' said the patient, 'bit I'm maist damnable thirsty. I cwid dee fine wi a drink o waater.'

'Weel,' said our surgeon of the North-east, responding in the patient's vernacular, 'If ye can jist hing on a meenitie. Ye see, ivnoo we've got nae wye ti pit it.'

IAN MIDDLETON, of Arradoul, near Buckie, recalled a spell in hospital at Aberdeen Royal Infirmary. Lying in the next bed was Wullie, from Strichen, who had fractured his hip.

To keep any unnecessary weight off his legs, a cage was put over them with the downie on top. Coming out of the anaesthetic, he was extremely raivelt and Ian had to call for the nurse when Wullie started to crank his legs at an alarming rate.

'What's the matter, Wullie?' asked the nurse.

'I canna get tae Strichen,' said Wullie. 'There's nae pedals in this bugger o a thing.'

WHEN YOUR co-author who works for the daily paper was visiting his mother during a rare spell in hospital, he found himself intrigued by the occupant of the next bed, an elderly lady from one of the tiny fisher villages between Fraserburgh and Peterhead.

We'll call her Elsie to protect her identity, but she was an absolute charmer.

'Fit div ye think I'm in for?' she asked him one evening.

He shrugged his shoulders.

'Weel, it's nae that,' she said, pointing at the cage over her lower legs. 'That's twa broken legs, that.'

'But you say you're not in for those,' he said.

'No,' she said. 'That broken legs happened in the operatin theeter. I went doon and ma legs wis a'richt. I come back and they wis baith broken. I'm sure they drappit me aff the table.'

'That's terrible.'

'Of coorse it's terrible. And me in the hospital, tee. Ye dinna expect ti get yer legs broke in a hospital, div ye? Nae baith o them, onywye. Waur nor that, I gied doon ti get ma appendix oot and fin I come back and the gas wore aff there's a notie waitin for me fae the surgeon sayin that they'd found something else in ma intimmers fin they wis pokin aboot, but seein as I hidna gien ma consint for onything abeen ma appendix, they couldna dee nithing aboot it til I signed on the dottit line. So they jist shooed me back up and sent me a notie. Hiv ye ivver heard the like? I mean, they wis pokin aboot inside me fitivver; I widna hiv mindit gettin the hale jing-bang deen a at the same time.

'So here I am, back up in this bed wi twa broken legs, recovering fae gettin ma appendix wheepit oot and noo I'm waitin for anither operation that I didna even ken I needit.'

She sank back on her pillows, exhausted with the exertions of her story.

Then she looked up again: 'I wis near a'richt fin I come in here,' she said. 'I'll be gaun hame a bliddy wreck.'

A FEW misunderstandings from the files of patients' reports, as told to us by a receptionist at Aberdeen Royal Infirmary. Transcribing from the dictaphone to typewritten words can be tricky sometimes.

'The patient was admitted for high thigh amputation.'

appeared as
'The patient came in for Hi-Fi amputation.'

'Cystoscope passed easily.'
was translated as
'Sister Cope passed easily.'

'The abdomen was opened and there was pus.'
appeared as
'The abdomen was opened and there was puss.'

'Her mouth, tongue and fauces were healthy.'
became
'Her mouth, tongue and falsies were healthy.'

Law and Order

We have included this chapter to prove that even lawyers, judges and policemen have a sense of humour. Unfortunately, the planned chapter on accountants had to go by the board.

ONE ABERDEEN lawyer between the wars used to tell a deliciously self-deprecating story of walking down Union Street, Aberdeen, with his wife one Sunday when a voluptuous young blonde whom he had managed to defend successfully in court, shouted and waved a cheery wave and blew him a kiss across the street.

He waved back before he realised that his wife was glowering.

'She was that case a few months back,' he said hastily. 'And before you ask it was purely a professional relationship.'

'Aye,' said his wife. 'Your profession or hers?'

SHERIFF MUIR Russell was one of the more entertaining dispensers of justice at Aberdeen Sheriff Court. On one occasion, passing a sentence of two years' imprisonment on a notorious old thief and drunk in his seventies, the guilty man wailed: 'I'll nivver live ti finish twa years ma lord.'

'Never mind,' said Sheriff Russell. 'Just you do what you can.'

SHERIFF RUSSELL was also in situ when a young hooligan was being fined £50 for breaking the peace. 'Do you need time to pay?' inquired the sheriff.

The youth, either sullen or unable to understand the question, stood there glowering silently.

'Do you need time to pay your fine in instalments?' inquired Sheriff Russell again.

The youth stood in glum silence.

Eventually, the sheriff addressed the court. 'Is there

anyone present who can speak for this young man?' A middle-aged man in anorak and jeans stood and raised his hand. 'I'm his da, yer lordship.' Sheriff Russell beckoned him down and the man stood beside his son.

'I was asking,' said Sheriff Russell, 'if your son needed time to pay his fine in instalments. I shall assume that he does. Now, would five pounds per week be in order?'

The man and his son went into a huddle of intense discussion, which broke a few seconds later and the father announced: 'No, yer lordship, not acceptable. I'm sorry.'

'What?' said Sheriff Russell, 'an apprentice tradesman with a reputable city firm and he can't manage five pounds a week? Why ever not?'

'Be fair, sir,' said the father. 'Fags and drink's an affa price nooadays.'

ONE BRIGHT spark at the Tulliallan Police College was asked what action he would take to help disperse a crowd.

'Well,' he said. 'In Aiberdeen, we'd start a collection.'

IN THE 1940s, James Simpson, a Banff solicitor, had an office at Foggieloan, where he did a few hours' consulting each week. A Foggie couple called one afternoon to arrange a defence on a charge of poultry-stealing. They sat down and gave an account of the incident, which Mr Simpson began to ponder.

He sat pensively with his elbows on the desk and his head cupped in his hands, eyes closed, considering the best course of action. He must have been sitting that way for a good few minutes – certainly longer than he realised – because he was startled to hear the wife say:

'Come on hame, Jim. The bugger's sleepin.'

MARY HAD a shoppie in a small Buchan village. One night, it was raided and the drawers ransacked. The village bobby arrived the following morning to make inquiries and, not noted for his sensitivity, asked: 'Weel, Mary, so somebody wis interferin wi yer drawers last nicht, eh?'

TWO BOBBIES were attending a road accident at a country crossroads which, in those days, was bounded on all sides by drystane dykes. The driver of one car, an old Austin Seven, said he had not seen the other car coming because of the height of the dyke.

The bobby was suspicious, and thought that the driver should certainly have been able to see the other car coming, because the driver's seat in an Austin Seven was not that low. But how could he prove it?

Shortly, he hit on a plan. He squatted down in the middle of the road and said to his colleague: 'Measure the distance fae the grun til my erse, then we'll measure the hicht o his seat fae the grun. Then we'll fin oot whither he saw the car or no.'

MANY YEARS ago, there worked in Aberdeen a police inspector who stood no nonsense from lower ranks and who never missed an opportunity to put them on the spot. One day, he was out in a patrol car with his driver, as well as a crewman and beatman in the back seat.

A call came over the radio. 'Control calling East Car! Control calling East Car! Go right away to the Boathouse Briggie. There's kids throwing stones at the trains.'

'Roger,' said the inspector.

Eager to impress his three colleagues with his knowledge of the city, he asked the driver: 'Do you know where the Boathouse Briggie is?'

'No,' said the driver, honestly.

He turned to the crewman. 'Do you?'

'No, sir.'

He turned to Peter, the beatman, convinced that total victory would soon be his. 'And you, Peter? Do you know where the Boathouse Briggie is?'

'Aye,' said Peter.

A fleeting look of disappointment crossed the inspector's face. 'Far is it, than?'

'It's far the kids is throwin steens at the trains.'

CONGRATULATIONS TO John Stewart, formerly of Grampian Police, who had the guts to tell a fine story against himself. When he was a beat bobby in the Mastrick and Northfield districts of Aberdeen, he covered his area on a bike – a great, black monster of a bike, he reports, with a seat like a Fordson Tractor.

One snowy day, he was cycling round the Cornhill prefabs and noticed a group of children enjoying themselves sledging down a short slope. However, John spotted that the slope ended beside a busy road, and he was concerned that an accident would occur.

He rode his big, black cycle towards them, intending to point out the dangers very gently. When he was about twenty yards from them, they became aware of him, stopped their sledging and gathered into a little guilty huddle at the foot of the icy slope.

'Now, kids,' he shouted, still cycling. 'You shouldn't be sledging here. It's dangerous.'

At the precise moment of uttering the word 'dangerous', the bike skidded from under him and he travelled the last few yards flat on his back and into the group of children. He looked up at a sea of frightened and innocent faces. And all he could think of to say was:

'Ye see fit I mean?'

BOB MILNE was butcher at Dunecht for many years and ran three vans delivering all round the area. He was out in one of them every day of the week, and it meant long hours. As is the way of country mobile shoppies, he was more than just a butcher; he carried news and did messages and all sorts of other community good deeds that go unsung too often. As a genial character, he was often invited into homes for a fly cup and news, or perhaps something stronger in the bitter days of winter.

There was a by-law at the time that prevented a vanman blowing his whistle to give notice of his arrival after 8pm. The Echt bobby had warned Bob many times, but Bob needed to speed up his rounds late in the day and the whistle was the only way to do it.

One night at Echt, Bob fussled his fussle once too often and the bobby stormed out of the station and up to the van: 'Dammit, butcher,' he said, 'I've tellt ye again and again tae tak that infernal fussle oot o yer moo at this time o nicht, and eneuch's eneuch. I maun chairge ye.'

An hour later, Bob was still delivering, this time at Midmar, just two or three miles up the road from Echt. The last delivery was a parcel of beef to the hostelry at Midmar – at the time licensed only for beer. As usual, Bob made his way into the kitchen for his nightcap to find the self-same bobby plunkit down at the table, diced cap on his knee and a liberal dram of whisky in his hand.

Revenge, when it comes, comes swiftly.

'Aye, aye, bobby,' said Bob. 'I didna ken the law allowed ye ti drink fusky in a porter and ale hoose.'

Bob was never charged.

IT'S A hot day at Aberdeen Beach and one bobby is striding along the Esplanade licking surreptitiously at an ice-cream cappie while enjoying the balmy breezes. Unfortunately for him and for his career prospects, the inspector is out on the prowl and spots his constable in a near-deserted part of the Esplanade carrying an ice-cream cone.

He directs the driver to draw up beside the constable.

'Now, min,' said the inspector. 'Ye ken fine ye shouldna be aetin an ice-cream on duty. I dinna care foo het it is. And fit the hell are ye deein awa up at this end, onywye? There's nithing up here. You should be doon at the ither end, in amon the folk, spikkin til them and makkin yersel seen.'

'Oh, aye, sir,' said the bobby, licking the rapidly melting remains of his ice-cream while being reprimanded. 'I tak yer pint. Fairly that. Aye.'

'Well, than, awa ye go,' said the inspector. 'And dinna let it happen again, or we'll hae ti see aboot it, and I'll mind on this caper the day wi yer ice-cream.'

'Aye, sir,' said the bobby. 'Fairly that. I tak yer pint.'

Then the bobby stopped. 'Eh, there's jist ae thing, sir.'

'And fit's that?' said the inspector.

The bobby popped the last of the cone into his mouth and swallowed it.

'Far's yer evidence?'

THERE IS a hardy annual story among the boys and girls in blue at Grampian Police of the slow-witted North-east cadet sent off for training to the police college. He was struggling with the phonetic alphabet (A Alpha, B Bravo, C Charlie, and so on), and was asked in a rapid-fire, random question session in class what the E stood for.

Quick as a flash, he shouted: 'Aeple.'

THE LAST winter before the Kittybrewster Mart closed in Aberdeen, two farmers from Insch and Kennethmont were heard discussing how sharp the frosts had been, and the Insch man wondered if this wasn't the coldest winter they could remember?

'Nivver,' said the Kennethmont man, 'div ye nae mind the winter o 1947?'

'Wis it caul?'

'Caul? I'll say it wis caul. Ma wife saw twa solicitors walkin doon Union Street and they'd their hands in their ain pooches.'

. . . and from *Anither Dash o Doric*

YOU CAN'T help feeling sorry for Abbie Innes, of Aberdeen, who drove to Glasgow for the first time in 1989 and admits that he must have been travelling just a shade over the speed limit when a flashing blue light appeared in his rear-view mirror.

He pulled over to the side and waited for the traffic officer to appear at his window. The officer duly appeared and invited Abbie for a discussion in the back seat of the patrol car.

Facing incredible odds, our North-east man decided to lay on the Doric as broadly as he could, hoping to touch the bobby's heart with the plight of an obvious country bumpkin bewildered in the big city.

'I didna ken fit yer signs meant, ye see,' he said, adding by way of explanation: 'I'm fae Aiberdeen.'

'Well, sir,' said the bobby, 'funnily enough, the signs mean the same doon here as they mean in Aberdeen.'

JIMMY IRVINE, who retired to a croft near Banff, recalls his days as a travelling salesman and being stopped for speeding between Inverurie and Huntly.

The traffic officer read him the charge and asked if he had anything to say. Jimmy thought it might help his case if he explained how many miles he travelled, in perfect safety, every year.

'Ye ken this,' he said, 'I've driven a ower the country since 1953, maybe thirty – forty-thoosan mile a year, and this is the first time I've been stoppit.'

The bobby looked decidedly underwhelmed.

'In that case,' he said, 'we should hiv stoppit ye a lang time ago.'

A HARASSED mother arrived at Lumsden police station to complain about her own son, who was getting more than a little out of hand.

'He jist winna dee fit he's tell't,' she said.

She asked the bobby if he would maybe turn up at their house some night and speak to the young rascal in the hope that that might give him 'a dasht good scare'.

'Eer face is as ugly's mine,' said our country constable. 'Awa hame and scare him yersel.'

JIMMY WAS the old-style bobby nearing the end of his service to the community in the old Moray and Nairn

Constabulary. He maybe wasn't among the ranks of the new liberated thinkers, but his philosophy was that you couldn't teach old dogs or cops new tricks.

He had risen through the ranks to Inspector with his honest-to-goodness approach and might well have been the originator of the E for Aeple callsign we highlighted in *A Dash o Doric*.

The patrol car with Inspector Jimmy (we hide his real identity) and Constable John was on Harbour Street, Nairn, when Jimmy thought it was time to report in.

'Car twenty-seven to Echo. Am patrolling north on Harbour Street, Nairn, and approaching the harbour.'

Back came an unidentified voice to an unamused inspector:

'Haud gyan.'

FROM THE same branch of Her Majesty's Constabulary, we heard of the superintendent who applied for a more senior post, listing among his qualifications that he had been dux of his school. One of his fellow-supers was heard to remark:

'Dux at his skweel? Goad Almichty: sivven pupils.'

IT WAS maybe this rival superintendent who was the main player in this next story.

Sandy was an extremely able policeman and came of a very old, established farming family. With his service years about up, he couldn't wait to get his police pension and head back to the family farm.

We speak of the days when all photography was done by the CID, including taking pictures at fatal road accidents. The photographs were then approved by the duty superintendent before being passed over to the fiscal.

On this occasion, a detective-sergeant went up with a batch of photographs of wreckage and general mayhem, some of which was on the roadway and some in an adjoining turnip field.

The superintendent studied the prints, going back to one

general view several times. Eventually he gave his verdict.
Handing this print back to the sergeant, he said:

'Man, isn't that a gran level park o neeps?'

WE ARE indebted to John Duff, that former policeman
and stalwart of the Braemar Mountain Rescue Team, for
this one and a few more on the subject of bobbies.

Former Chief Inspector Peter MacInnes came straight from
his native Skye to be the first recruit to the Scottish North-
eastern Counties Constabulary when it was formed in 1949.

All recruits were stationed at headquarters at Banff until
they were allocated to a station. During this waiting period,
Peter heard some bloodcurdling stories about the poor
bobby who had been posted to Foggieloan.

In due course, Peter learned that he was to be stationed at
Aberchirder, and he turned to his neighbour and expressed
his heartfelt relief that he had managed to avoid that
terrible Foggieloan place.

THE LATE Tom Chasser was Chief Constable of the
County of Aberdeenshire from the late Fifties and was a
great supporter of the tradition and heritage of the area.

Lonach Gathering took pride of place as far as Highland gatherings were concerned and, as a most gifted
after-dinner speaker, he was invited as the main guest at
a Lonach Dinner.

In proposing the main toast, he bemused the loyal Men
o Lonach by stating that he hadn't realised that the Gaelic
tongue was still alive in the strath. Actually, the last
native-born Gaelic speaker from those parts had died a
good few years previously, but Tom went on to explain
his remarks.

Approaching Strathdon with time to spare, he had asked
his driver to call in past the Glenkindie Hotel. It was a
terrible night of rain and, as he had entered the front door,
he had encountered a lad soaked to the skin, parking his
cycle by the side of the porch.

They exchanged greetings and, approaching the bar, our Chief Constable was compelled to ask the barman if, indeed, Gaelic was still spoken.

'Oh, there's naebody spikks the Gaelic here,' responded the man behind the counter, to which Tom replied:

'That's strange; when I spoke to that lad at the door he said: "Hooer anicht."'

THE OLD Banffshire Force seemed to produce more characters than the others, possibly because of the number of stills – official and illicit – in the area.

One such bobby was Jimmy Mackie, stationed latterly at Ballindalloch. He and John 'Black Jock' Mowat had joined together in the early Thirties.

Jimmy was to remain unpromoted, although not for lack of native guile, while John rose to become a superintendent and later Deputy Chief Constable.

In the course of his duties as the Deputy Chief, John had occasion to visit Ballindalloch, arriving just as Jimmy had the beets slackened, feet up and was having his post-lunch snooze.

Answering the office doorbell while pulling on his tunic, and not that pleased with the interruption, he saw who his caller was.

He glowered at the DCC.

'Weel,' he barked. 'Are ye Superintendent Mowat the day or are ye jist Jock?'

WE THANK John Duff again for this one showing how quick wit and a certain amount of low cunning can come in handy in the police force.

An Aberlour PC was not found wanting one Games day when, in the course of duty (what else?), he had taken maybe one or two drams too many.

He was seen by a senior officer feeling his way round the rope at the edge of the arena, trying to steady himself. Summoned to account for his actions, he replied:

'Sir, I wis jist feelin the rope in case some o yon young buggers o loons hid cut it.'

TOM CHASSER also told the following story against himself which he swore was true. It might just have been, and it happened soon after his arrival as Chief Constable in the North-east.

Visiting a function one night out of uniform in one of the larger burghs in the force area, he decided to go for a quick stroll and soon came on a bobby in a shop doorway having a quick draw on a fag.

Standing in beside the bobby, he made conversation, realising that he had not been recognised. After a few moments he introduced himself as the Chief Constable, but was totally unprepared for the reply.

Unimpressed, his shop-front companion said:

'Weel, ye've got yersel a damnt fine job.'

THE LATE Willie Merrilees was Lothian Chief Constable in the 1950s and was a great fisherman who liked to venture out on the Spey whenever he found himself with a little spare time. One year, his usual hotel at Grantown was fully booked, so he checked into a smaller, but very comfortable, hotel with its own bar.

As a resident, he could drink there all day and all night if he wanted, but he noticed after a few days that the bar was doing a lively trade among people he suspected were Grantown folk. The locals were dropping in without question.

Purely in a spirit of inquiry, Willie happened to ask the landlord: 'What time do you usually close the bar here?'

'It depends on the fishin,' said the landlord, 'bit usually aboot the end o October.'

Please, Miss

Of all the professions, the one that has the most profound effect on any community is the teacher. Teacher's grip lasts a lifetime, well after the confines of the classroom. But even teachers have a sense of humour. In fact, it's probably a professional necessity.

A TEACHER who spent a large part of his career at Ellon Academy recalls marking an exercise in which one of the questions had been: 'What is rabies and what can you do about it?'

One answer was: 'Rabies is Jewish ministers. You can't do anything about it.'

A PRIMARY teacher in a North-east rural school was having terrible trouble stopping one of her broader-spoken pupils from using the word 'putten' when, as we all know, the word is 'put'.

To correct him once and for all, she wrote on the board:

I have just putten on my shoes

. . . then asked him if he saw anything wrong with the sentence.

'Aye,' he said confidently, 'ye've gaen and putten putten far ye should hiv putten put.'

A TEACHER at a primary school in Upper Donside was having quite a job persuading one young farmer's son to speak English and not lapse into the Doric. The last straw came one afternoon when they were discussing parents' hobbies.

'Ma mither maks her ain wine,' he told the class. 'Bit she's hid ti stop for a file, for she hisna nae bottles.'

'No, no, no, no, no,' said the teacher, standing up. 'Not:

"She hisna nae bottles." It should be. "My mother has no bottles." Now, start again.'

He began again, treading a little more warily. 'My mother makes wine but she has had to stop for a while because she has no bottles.'

'Much better,' said the teacher approvingly. 'Anything else?'

'Aye,' said the boy. 'She's gey ticht for corks, tee.'

TWIN brothers were sitting in a circle of fellow-pupils during a primary-school reading lesson. They stuck at the word GRACE. The teacher tried to coax one of them out of the stall, saying: 'Come on, now, Robbie. What does your father say before a meal?'

Robbie looked at Frankie and Frankie looked at Robbie.

Robbie looked at the teacher. 'Please, miss, ma faither says: "Robbie and Frunkie, blaa yer noses."'

MISS MACKIE taught near Monymusk in the early 1950s and was annoyed one day when two small brothers turned up late for school. Miss Mackie asked the older one why.

'Well, Miss,' he said, 'I was half-way to the school but I took an awful sair belly and had to run intil the woods.'

'I see,' said Miss Mackie, turning to the smaller boy, 'and what about you, Sandy, did you have a sore stomach, too?'

'No, miss,' said Sandy, 'bit I hid ti pu the grass.'

MANY YEARS ago, the bakery at Tarland was Grant's the Bakers. The infant class at school were working their way through a lesson about animal noises. The cow moos. The sheep baas, the pig grunts.

'Now,' said the teacher, 'does anyone have a story about moos, or baas or grunts?'

'Please, miss,' said one lad, 'I get ma playpiece fae Grunts.'

JAMES MICHIE, long-time director of education in Aberdeenshire and then for Grampian Region, and an ardent proponent of the Doric, tells a delicious story of paying an official visit to Braemar Primary School and accepting the teacher's offer of keeping his hand in by teaching a class of eight-year-olds for a short time.

Mr Michie enjoyed the 40 minutes back at the blackboard thoroughly, and asked the boys and girls if they had, too.

'Oh, yes, sir,' they chorused.

Mr Michie thanked them all and began walking towards the classroom door when a small voice piped from the back: 'Hey, min, ye're awa wi wir chalk.'

AT THE handwork class, a teacher not from the North-east was having difficulty getting the boys, in particular, to hurry up making placemats by threading laces through holes in pieces of card.

Eventually, she said: 'Come on, Ian; hurry up threading that lace through those holes.'

Ian looked at her thoughtfully. 'That's nae lace. That's pints.'

THE SAME Ian was listening to the same teacher telling the Bible story about the lost sheep. She told the class that the wee lamb had said to itself that it would leave the other lambs and go on to the rocks and explore, and that was why it got lost. 'Now,' she said to the class, 'what do you think of that?'

'I dinna believe it,' said Ian. 'Sheep canna spik.'

AT GALLOWHILL School, a small boy wandered into the headmaster's room. 'Are ee the dominie, sir?'

'I am.'

'Div you ken this: the grieve shot oor cat last nicht.'

'Oh, my, that's a terrible shame. Did you cry?'

'Fit wid I dee that for? It wis the cat he shot, nae me.'

PUPILS ARRIVED at Rhynie School as usual one morning and sat down in their usual places, except for one older boy who stood. The teacher told him to sit down.

He said he couldn't, because 'if ee'd a blin lump on yer erse as I hiv, ee'd be gled ti stan, tee.'

FORMER TEACHER turned writer Lilianne Grant Rich tells of six-year-old Robbie, who came from one of the outlying crofts and had to walk two miles to school and two miles back every day. Lilianne was in no doubt that Robbie was turned out impeccably by his mother every morning but, by the time he had investigated all the dykes and burns and ditches on the two miles, he arrived always in need of a good encounter with soap and water.

Although he said nothing, Robbie's face for the first few mornings in Lilianne's class indicated that he regarded the calling of the class roll a daft-like ploy and that he, for one, would have nothing to do with it if at all possible.

For a week, Lilianne ignored it, thinking that he would soon feel left out and would want to join in like the others.

Then, one day, she called his name three times, fixing him with a stare.

Eventually, and extremely reluctantly, Robbie said: 'Present.'

Lilianne noted it with satisfaction.

'Aye,' said Robbie, 'bit ye saw me a the time.'

THE SAME Robbie was in class one wintry morning during hymn-singing. As Lilianne played piano, Robbie rose from his seat and strode over to the classroom fire and stretched his hands to the blaze.

She took no notice for a few moments, but eventually stopped in mid-verse and looked towards him inquiringly.

A few moments later, Robbie realised she had stopped playing. He gave her a brief glance over his right shoulder and said, in a completely matter-of-fact and reassuring way: 'Aye, on ye go wi yer playin. Nivver heed me. I'm fair frozen.'

ROBBIE HAD difficulty with arithmetic, and no matter how Lilianne tried to explain to him that a number subtracted from itself left nothing, he couldn't grasp it at all. She tried counters, dots and fingers, but it just wouldn't sink in. Eventually, summoning another waucht of patience, she said: 'Now, Robbie, we'll pretend it's market day. You have six pigs at home and I'm going to take a lorry and take six pigs away. How many would be left?'

At last, a look of radiant understanding illuminated Robbie's face. 'Man,' he said, 'that wid be gran. There wid be neen left, and I could bide in ma bed til eicht ilky mornin, for I wid hae nithing ti feed bit masel and ma rubbits.'

ONE WEEK, Robbie arrived late every morning, and Lilianne began to wonder if he was taking a dislike to school. As the bairns were leaving for home on the Friday afternoon, she said with a laugh: 'Well, Robbie, do you think you'll be on time for school on Monday?'

'No, I dinna think so,' he said. 'Ye see, I *div* like ti come in late and get a "Good Morning, Robbie" a til masel.'

IN ANOTHER of Lilianne's classes was Jean, a small chatterbox, almost to the point of disruption. In those days, removal of tonsils and adenoids was not as common as it is today and Jean went round bragging about her forthcoming visit to hospital. Some weeks later, she was back in her usual place, blethering non-stop.

Sandy, who shared her desk, looked up imploringly at

Lilianne and said with a sigh that indicated real disappointment: 'Yon doctor mannie maybe took Jean's tonsils awa,
bit I'll sweir he nivver took her tongue.'

ONE MONTH, the headmaster delivered the teachers' pay
cheques personally, and laid Lilianne's on her desk.
    Billy interrupted. 'That's yer pey, isn't it?'
    Lilianne just nodded.
    Billy thought for a few moments more. 'My dad gies me
tippence a wikk. Foo muckle dis he (with a jerk of his head
towards the headmaster) gie you?'

LILIANNE ADMITTED to the butterflies all teachers
experience when HM Inspectorate pays a visit to the
classroom, but was charmed when six-year-old Valerie
was standing beside one inspector, reading to him, when
the inspector took hold of one of her gorgeous red curls
and pretended to cut it off and put it in his pocket.
    Valerie laid down her book and contemplated him closely
for a moment. Then, taking him by both lapels, she gave him
a gentle shake and said: 'Oh, my! Fit'll we dee wi this great
big coorse loon?'

DAISY WISEMAN was a teacher at Folla Rule School
between the wars and used to tell of a farmer's son,
Jimmy Grant, who was among the new intake listening
to her explaining about the standards of behaviour she
would expect from them.
    Suddenly, Jimmy rose from his seat and stamped towards
the door. 'And where might you be going?' asked his
teacher.
    'Nivver you mind,' said Jimmy. 'I'll be back in twa
ticks.'
    Sure enough, Jimmy was back two minutes later and said
to Miss Wiseman.
    ''At's better. I wis fair burstin.'

AT WOODLANDS School on Lower Deeside in 1944, the class was having a geography lesson from their teacher, Miss Spark, when the dominie, Mr McKelvie, appeared and said to one pupil: 'Geography is it, James? All right, then, can you tell me what a cape is?'

'Yes, sir,' said James. 'It's a cap ye weir on yer heid.'

IT WAS coming up for the annual school concert at a Buchan primary school. We believe it was at Longside, but we can't be absolutely certain. The teacher in Primary One was holding informal auditions for a farmyard scene as a backdrop to the nativity play.

'Now, who can do farmyard noises?'

Up shot a few eager hands. 'Please, miss, I can moo,' said Jean.

'I can clock lik a hen,' said Annie.

'Me, miss! I can grunt lik a pig,' cried Airchie.

'And I can baa,' said Tommy.

Then up shot the hand of wee Johnnie, whose domain was his father's farm.

'All right, Johnnie,' said the teacher. 'Let's hear your farmyard noise.'

'Get aff that bliddy tractor!'

SOMETIMES, TEACHERS don't get the answers they expect. One woman in charge of a primary class, who asked not to be named or credited, asked in the late 1940s for a sentence using the word 'exaggeration'.

A hand went up. 'Please, miss, my faither says ye're guid-lookin, bit ma mither says that's an exaggeration.'

. . . and from *Anither Dash o Doric*

BILL SHAND, now living in the Highlands, retired as an English teacher at a large North-east comprehensive in

1992 and took with him forty years of memories, particularly of exam-paper blunders. Four of his favourites were:

What caused the Depression?

Lots of people being depressed because they hadn't any money.

and

What is the correct name for your father's father?

George.

and

When we say an animal is sure-footed, what does that mean?

Every time it kicks you, it never misses.

and

Define the term 'circle'.

A circle is a round line with no kinks or corners, joined up again so that you can't tell where it started.

AND FROM Banff Academy:

Ferdinand Magellan circumcised the world with a 200ft clipper.

AND IN the mid-1970s a terse telephone call from an angry parent reached Inverurie Academy. The man was outraged that his offspring's illness should be queried by a suspicious teacher, who had demanded further information:

'Foo wid I ken fit's wrang with ma loon?' he demanded. 'And foo wid I ken fan he'll be back? I'm nae Houdini.'

VIOLET THOMSON was a primary teacher at a rural Buchan school in the mid-1960s and had decided to teach a lesson on weather. After discussing rain, snow and sunshine, she moved on to the topic of thunder and lightning. She asked for someone to explain how they thought thunder and lightning happened.

There was a long silence until eight-year-old Victor, whose domain was his father's farm, shot up a brosey arm.

'Yes, Victor?'

'Please, Miss,' drawled Victor, 'ma mither says it's the Baby Jesus playin wi the licht switch and God giein him a skelpit erse.'

MISS THOMSON also recalls teaching a class of eight-year-olds at a school in rural Strathbogie in the late 1950s when the subject for the afternoon was mental arithmetic. Willie was not a particularly quick thinker at the best of times, but when asked to add nine and seven he was thoroughly stumped.

'Is it eichteen, miss?' he asked.

'Now, now, Willie,' she said gently. 'You're just guessing.'

'Sivventeen?'

'Enough of that, now. You know perfectly well nine and seven are sixteen.'

Miss Thomson said she was about to move on to the next sum, but had to turn to the blackboard to stifle a smile when, out of the corner of her eye, she saw Willie lean to the boy next to him and whisper: 'What a bliddy caper. She said *eicht* and *eicht* wis sixteen.'

TO KEITH Grammar School, where a first-year pupil was struggling badly with a problem of geometry. No matter how hard he tried, Sandy couldn't make head nor tail of the odd-looking shape on the paper in front of him.

'Come on, Sandy,' said his teacher. 'You know how to work out the area of odd-looking shapes. You break down the shape into littler shapes that are easier to work out, like squares and triangles, and then you add it all up and you've got the total area.'

Sandy scratched his head and looked as blank as ever.

'All right,' said his teacher, trying a new tack. 'You're a farmer's son.'

Sandy's chest puffed out. 'Ay,' he said proudly.

'All right, so imagine this shape is one of your father's parks. If you draw a line here . . . and here . . . you're left with a rectangle, a long thin triangle on one side and a short fat triangle on the other.'

Sandy looked as if the fog might be clearing.

'So work out the sizes of the rectangle and the two triangles for me and you've got the area of the park.'

Sandy set about the task with renewed vigour. After five minutes he shouted the teacher back and showed her his answer. It was correct and he beamed with pride, then added: 'Bit what a helluva aakward park ti ploo.'

A CHEMISTRY class at Turriff Academy in the mid-1960s was discussing the metal-eating properties of acid. The teacher had dropped a succession of small bits of metal into a beaker of sulphuric acid and the class had watched the metals fizz and dissolve, or burst into flames, or sputter round the surface before disappearing.

Finally, the teacher fumbled in his pocket and pulled out a half-crown.

'Now,' he said, 'here's a half-crown. I'm going to drop it into the acid. Will it dissolve?'

There was a short silence while the class considered the proposal, then Leslie put up his hand.

'Yes, Leslie?'

'No, sir, it winna.'

'And can you explain to the rest of the class why not?'

'Because if it wid, ye widna drap it in the acid.'

OUR SAME source told us of a history class when he was a student teacher at Aberdeen Grammar School. They were discussing the line of succession to the English royal family and had reached Edward VI.

'All right,' he said. 'Queen Mary followed Edward VI, but who followed Mary?'

There was a lot of deep thinking, but a wag at the back of class said: 'Her little lamb.'

WE'VE TO thank Lorna Alexander, of Glenkindie, for this

tale of rural schooling in Upper Donside. When Lorna was teaching at Strathdon School, there was a nasty bug on the go and she was feeling decidedly ropey herself.

After returning from the latest of many dashes to the toilet to be sick, a wee lad (one of a big family) put his arms round about her and said soothingly:

'Nivver mind, teacher. Gwa and hae a lie-doon a filie. My mam wis sick es mornin, tee. Dad says it'll be anither bliddy bairn.

'He disna ken foo she manages it.'

THE FRENCH teacher at one prominent North-east grammar school was not having a good day and the class was not responding to her efforts to translate to French.

It was a basic first-week or second-week lesson.

'When I say: "Bonjour, mes enfants," I want your response: "Bonjour, Mademoiselle."'

This was done parrot-fashion in unison, but to find if the message had got through, Mademoiselle decided to try the individual pupils.

She was pleased to see that the teaching appeared to have had its effect – until she came to little Paul.

'Bonjour, mon enfant.'

'Bonjour Madame-yersel.'

PETER SLATER, of Brechin, tells of his wife's cousin, Betty Craig, who was headmistress at Rhynie. She was teaching the young bairns the poem of 'Young Lochinvar' and reached the line: 'Boatman do not tarry.'

Miss Craig paused and asked: 'What does "tarry" mean?'

James shot his hand up.

'Please miss, I ken. It means "dinna scutter".'

Good for the Soul

Between tending to the spiritual needs of their North-east flocks, men (and women) of the cloth have had the odd moment to jot down a few of the more lightsome encounters of their careers. Evidently, dog-collar and wicked sense of humour are not mutually exclusive.

A KINCARDINE minister was also a keen golfer and had accepted an invitation for a Saturday round of golf at Inverurie. Unfortunately, the minister was playing very badly and was becoming more and more frustrated until, by the time he missed an easy putt at the 14th, he could contain himself no longer and let go a minor expletive or two.

His golfing chum – also a member of his flock – was mildly shocked that a man of the cloth had such a ripe vocabulary, and said as much.

'You're quite right, of course, Peter,' said the minister. 'In fact, I've been thinking for a while that I'm going to have to give up the whole thing. It's just getting too frustrating for me.'

The chum was just as horrified. 'Michty,' he said, 'surely ye widna gie up yer golf?'

'Certainly not,' said the minister. 'I meant the ministry.'

OLD MAGGIE had forgotten to put her clock forward an hour at the end of March and arrived an hour late at the kirk. She stepped down the aisle in a fine new hat just as the minister raised his arms and pronounced: 'Jesus Christ! Hallelujah!' at the end of the service. Maggie about-turned and marched out.

The minister became worried when Maggie did not turn up for the next few weeks, so he visited her and asked why she wasn't in church these days.

'Weel, minister,' she said, 'the last time I turned up ye raised yer hauns and cried: "Jesus Christ, I hardly knew ye!" and that wis an affa thing to say aboot ma new hat.'

ONE WEARY minister at Forglen had noted that a spate of break-ins around the parish had happened over the weekend and had caused great concern. After the Sunday service, he was chatting to parishioners when one elder asked: 'What would you do, minister, if someone broke into the manse one night looking for money?'

'Well,' said the minister, 'I'd rise and help him.'

A FORMER prison chaplain at Peterhead noticed that one of the prisoners never received any visitors and, as the weeks wore on, began to feel mightily sorry for him.

'Tell me, Jim,' he said one day. 'I notice that nobody ever comes to visit you. Have you no friends or family?'

'Aye,' said Jim, 'bit they're a in the jile, as weel.'

A COUNTRY woman who had moved into a granite villa in the West End of Aberdeen after her husband had shown a talent at playing the stock market was about to be visited by the new minister. Unfortunately, a gang of ruffians was playing about in the street outside.

The lads began taunting the minister for his odd style of dress and for having a very old car. The minister (the man who wrote to tell us about the story) was quite amused by it and chose to sail through it towards the front door, but his hostess-to-be was horrified, and lost no time in telling the ruffians so.

Unfortunately, she made the common mistake of trying to pan-loaf it.

'You! You ruffians! Get away with you! Away home to your mithers! I'll call the police!'

Then she turned to the minister and apologised profusely. 'Come away inside for your tea, minister,' she advised, 'and don't bother your erse with them.'

THE MINISTER had been telling his Sunday School about the lost sheep and how Jesus had had ninety-nine of them, but had been distraught to have lost one and had been determined to find it.

'Now,' said the minister. 'It was very important to Jesus that he find the lost sheep, even although he had ninety-nine others. Does anybody know why?'

One wee lad from a nearby croft put up his hand and offered: 'It wid likely hae been the tup.'

A MINISTER in entirely another part of Aberdeenshire had been telling his Sunday School children about the importance of love against hate. 'Now,' he said, smiling, 'let's see if you can tell me the difference between love and hate. Can someone give me a sentence with the words Love and Hate in it?'

'Please, sir! Please, sir!'

'Yes, Willie, what's your sentence?'

'Please, sir! I love het pies!'

A VILLAGE worthy attending a funeral at Essil Church-yard, Garmouth, thanked the minister for the lovely address then, gathering himself up against the cold, sighed and said: 'Aye, I wid like fine to be beeried here in Essil. If I'm spared.'

ON A crowded railway carriage into Aberdeen in the late 1940s, a young minister was holding forth about how well he knew his Buchan parish. Somewhat ambitiously, he declared that he was sure he knew everything that was going on there.

An old chap leaned across and tapped him on the knee. 'Excuse me, meenister,' he said. 'I ken something ee dinna ken.'

'Really?' said the minister.

'Aye. My wife's yer washerwumman, and I'm weerin een o yer sarks.'

BEFORE THE war, in one particular North-east village was a garage staffed by a man called Bob who drove the village taxi and specialised in repairing bicycles. He also had an extremely pronounced stutter.

One night, the elderly village minister arrived with his equally elderly bike, wheeled it up beside the inspection pit and tapped Bob on the shoulder.

'Robert,' he said, 'would you have an old seat for my bicycle?'

Without turning round, Bob replied: 'Fit wye? Is the bu- bu- bugger ye've got nae aul enough?'

A RUNDOWN croft in the heart of Buchan was the home of Mrs Eppie McIntosh, her hens, her cows and her numerous cats who had the run of the house. Seeing the minister coming up the road towards the croft, presumably on his annual visit, she had just enough time to stuff the scattered papers and clothes under the cushions and rush to the door to greet him.

'Gweed morning, minister. Come awa in.'

Having settled himself in a chair by the fire, scattering cats in all directions, he was asked by Eppie if he would like a cup of tea. He had been warned by the kirk session of Eppie's standards of hygiene, but he accepted, albeit reluctantly.

Through to the kitchen she went and came back with a cup which was accepted graciously. Thinking that maybe it hadn't been near a sink for a wee while, the minister turned it deftly round to the other side and took a sip, only to hear Eppie remark:

'Aye, meenister, I see ye're left-handit lik masel.'

A VISITOR to the country met up with a farmer from the area round Mormond Hill and, in the course of the conversation, asked to which church he belonged.

'Oh,' said the farmer, 'that aa depens far the waddin or the funeral's bein held.'

A COUNTRY minister was taking a morning walk and came upon one of his Sunday School pupils feeding the farm poultry.

'Are all these hens yours, Willie?' he asked.

'Yes, sir,' said Willie.

Just then, the cock started crowing.

'Now, Willie,' said the minister, 'when the cock crows in the morning, do you know what that is invariably a sign of?'

'Yes, sir,' said Willie. 'It's a sign he's nae sleepin.'

IN THE days when there were no such things as linked charges, and every country church had a minister of its own, three of the most remote ministers turned up at the quarterly presbytery meeting, began chatting and discovered that all their churches had bats. They began swapping tips on how to contain the problem, and perhaps even get rid of them.

'I did suggest to a farmer nearby that he might be able to shoot at the creatures as they came out at night,' said the first minister, 'but I must confess it was not the most efficient solution, and I do feel a little guilty about it.'

'We strung a strawberry net over the hole under the eaves where they were nesting,' said the second. 'It worked up to a point, but there were still one or two who were able to wriggle free.'

The third minister put down his cup of tea. 'Jist baptise them,' he said. 'Ye'll nivver see them again.'

A RETIRED Donside minister who asks not to be named says that he visited a sheltered-housing complex in 1992 to see one of his old parishioners, a spinster who had just reached her 100th birthday.

The conversation wore round to marriage, and the minister observed that she had never been courted or betrothed. Had she never thought that the companionship of wedlock would have been a comfort in her old age?

'Meenister,' she said, 'I'd a dog that snored, a lum that smoked and a cat that wis oot a nicht. Fit need hid I o a man?'

AFTER A wedding at Lumsden in the mid-1950s, the minister was doing the social rounds of the guests and came upon two Kildrummy worthies propping up the bar. Both of them were known for long marriages. Sandy, in fact, had celebrated his golden wedding not two weeks before.

'Well, Sandy,' said the minister, 'another happy day, eh? How does it make you feel seeing this young couple setting out on the long path that you've travelled yourself these last fifty years. They're in for a lot of happiness, eh?'

'Meenister,' said Sandy. 'Wullie and me here wis jist sayin we didna ken fit happiness wis until we got mairriet.'

'Aye,' said Wullie. 'And then it wis ower late.'

THE SAME minister reports that later at the same wedding reception he overheard Sandy and Wullie conversing with another Kildrummy farmer, when Sandy turned to Wullie and said: 'No, Sandy, like yersel, I couldna ask for a better wife.'

Then he took another sip of his dram. 'I'd like til,' he added, 'bit I widna dare.'

A MINISTER who preached once in the Church of Scotland in London in 1959 says that he noticed that there were three pennies in the collection plate and joked from the pulpit: 'I see there are three pennies in the collection this morning. We must have an Aberdonian in our midst.'

'No,' said an English voice. 'Three of them.'

BILL DUGUID was travelling by train from Maud to Aberdeen in 1938 and found himself seated next to what looked like a very stern-faced gentleman when a farmer in the seat opposite took out a bottle of whisky and began taking a swig.

The clergyman looked at the farmer disapprovingly. 'I'm sixty-five years old,' he said, 'and do you know I've never touched a drop of that awful stuff.'

'Aye, weel,' said the farmer, taking another swig. 'And ye winna be startin the day, eether.'

THE KIRK elders were not at all impressed with the sermon preached by the new minister, and said so to each other as they discussed it afterwards.

Opinions were many, but the general view was put most succinctly by the village grocer, who said: 'In the first place, he read it. In the second place, he didna read it weel. And in the third place, it wisna worth readin.'

. . . and from *Anither Dash o Doric*

KATHIE ROSS, of Fraserburgh, wrote to say that in the mid-1950s her English spinster aunt had spent a summer on their family farm near Lonmay. One morning, they had spotted the minister. Kathie's aunt had insisted on crossing the road to thank him for a light-hearted and thought-provoking sermon the previous Sunday.

In turn, he thanked her profusely and they chatted for a few minutes more.

'What really surprised me,' said Kathie's aunt, 'was the number of men in the congregation who went straight to the pub afterwards.'

'Ah, yes,' smiled the minister, 'the thirst after righteousness.'

THE REVEREND Gordon Smith, now retired to Aberdeen, was newly inducted to his Banffshire charge in the late 1940s and had been doing the rounds of his flock. As a single man at the time, he was usually invited to stay for his tea, an offer he accepted every time because the standard of rural fare was invariably excellent.

At one humble village home, he sat down with the family to a sumptuous repast, which was consumed in customary North-east silence.

After the last cup of tea, Mr Smith turned to the woman of the house and complimented her on her cooking. 'It's not often that I have a meal as wonderful as that,' he assured her.

The ten-year-old daughter looked at him and sighed: 'Neether div we.'

ETHEL BAIRD, of Kincorth, Aberdeen, was a Sunday School teacher at Stonehaven in the early 1960s and had been teaching a lesson about love and families. The assembly listened attentively – all apart from Arthur, aged eight, who was having none of it.

'I hate ma sister,' he informed Ethel vehemently. 'She's coorse.'

Ethel saw her chance. 'But you don't really mean that, Arthur,' she told him. 'You're maybe angry with her now and again but, mercy, all brothers and sisters have times like that. And always remember that God loves everybody.'

But Arthur remained determinedly unconvinced.

To break the logjam, Ethel suggested that all the class sit quietly and write a letter to God about someone in their families. That night, as she read through them, she came upon Arthur's letter. It began:

'Dear God, I no you love everbody, but yo've never met my sister.'

ETHEL ALSO recalls her cousin's family travelling from Stonehaven to Norfolk to attend the wedding of their son to a young Englishwoman. Also in the party was the groom's five-year-old sister.

When the choirboys entered in their flowing white robes, a five-year-old North-east voice filled the cathedral:

'Look, mam. They're a gaun ti get a haircut.'

ACCORDING TO the Rev. Charles Birnie, of Strichen, young Jeannie from a small croft up New Aberdour way was in an inquisitive mood, having been told of a distant family death.

'Mam, fin I ging ti Hivven, will Flossie get there as weel?'

'Oh aye, Jeannie; Flossie's a kindly doggie and she'll get there a richt.'

'An fit aboot Tiddles?'

'Oh aye, I'm sure yer wee cattie'll jine ye tee.'

'And Daisy the coo?'

'Oh weel, I'm nae sae sure there, dearie. Daisy's a muckle beast and there michtna be room for her in Hivven.'

A moment's hesitation, a puzzled look and Jeannie replied: 'Weel, fa's gyan tae hell for the milk?'

RETIRED TEACHER Lilianne Grant Rich has happy memories of childhood, but recalls a little puzzlement at Sunday School.

'I eest tae winner sair,' she recalled, 'fit wye the Gweed Lord preferred tae cut his walkin stick fae the rodden tree in preference tae ony ither trees roon aboot.

'I thocht that the bittie in the twinty-third psalm read:
Thy rodden staff me comfort still.'

SOME TIME in the Fifties, Pittodrie was booked for an evangelistic experience on a massive scale, with the appearance of America's disciple of God, Billy Graham.

The stadium was packed and, as at the usual football matches, refreshments of the soft nature were available at the start and at half-time.

A special busload attended from Culter, and Eileen McHardy recalled how she found it a most moving experience.

On the way home in the bus, she was contemplating the spiritual uplift of Billy Graham's message and the memorable singing of the choir, and the glory of God and how profound and soul-shaking an evening it had turned out to be, when she heard a rural wifie ask of her companion in the seat behind:

'Wis your pie affa satty?'

IN THE fishing villages of Inverallochy and Cairnbulg, the highlights of the year were the annual Temperance Walks, held on Christmas Day and New Year's Day. Homes were open to anyone who called, and they were invited to partake of the best of food and company. The days ended with the Walk Social, at which the best of the villages' amateur talent would play the flute, recite or sing the old gospel songs.

The village clergy would be there to have their say, and a chairman appointed by the walks committee would lead the evenings' entertainments.

One of the best known chairmen was Eddie Joe's Jockie (a name identifying him by his forebears). At one particular social, Jockie asked his committee in the back room: 'Is a the meenisters awa?'

'Aye.'

'Gran. We'll awa and tell lees.'

A STORY that predates the National Health Service came from the files of Professor Donald Francis Tovey, of Edinburgh. In the 1930s, the professor told often of the old minister on the Banffshire coast who would thunder and roar at his flock that every one of them would be sure to end in an eternal pit of damnation, a bottomless pit, where every last one of them would spend for ever weeping, wailing and gnashing their teeth.

Then he would pause, look round his congregation, see that most were elderly people and add:

'And for those of you without teeth, teeth will be provided.'

Mony a Gweed Tune

Yet again, one of the most fruitful sources of Doric humour has been the older generation. With far more years to call on, their reminiscences and stories are more varied, more numerous and often the most entertaining. It made it even more difficult for us to decide what to leave out.

BILL FROM Buckie was in his mid-seventies when he suffered a massive heart attack while walking in the town square. He was rushed to the local hospital and from there by ambulance to Aberdeen Royal Infirmary.

The event was the speak of the Banffshire coast for some days until it became clear that Bill would pull through and would soon be back at his regular seat in his favourite bar.

On the day that he was due to be discharged from the ARI, a nursing sister visited him just to be sure that he was happy about the changes to his way of life that he would have to make. Bill nodded solemnly throughout the lecture.

'But I don't want to suggest that it's all gloom and doom,' she concluded. 'I mean, a lot of heart-attack patients go to ridiculous lengths to keep as inactive as possible. They wrap themselves in cotton wool, which is almost as bad as going out disco-dancing. You mustn't be scared of physical exertion just because of one heart attack. Nowadays, we think regular light exercise is possibly the best way to a speedy recovery.

'Heavens, there's no reason why you shouldn't resume sexual relations as soon as you get home.'

Bill looked at her. 'I'm sivventy-six,' he said. 'Wid it be OK if I hid a cup o tea first?'

AN ELDERLY man from the heart of Aberdeenshire had decided to blow a substantial sum of money achieving his lifetime's ambition. He went on a Caribbean cruise and had a high old time, even although his thick country accent made communication difficult with a boatload of English, American, German, French and Canadian travellers.

At one port of call, many of the passengers were going ashore for a conducted tour when one man collapsed, unconscious, at the foot of the gangway. Heatstroke, was the verdict.

Our Aberdeenshire man, half-way back up the gangway, realised what was happening and was alarmed to see that the man had fallen very awkwardly, with one leg away to one side, his arms buckled under him and the other leg twisted to the left.

He knew enough about first aid to worry for the patient's comfort, and decided that the man had to be rearranged properly to make breathing easier. He had to be straightened out.

'Strachenimoot!' he cried. 'Strachenimoot!'

A ship's officer stopped him before he could reach the invalid. 'It's all right, sir,' he said. 'It's all right. Keep calm. We'll get you a German-speaking doctor.'

A TORPHINS woman was celebrating her 90th birthday but, unfortunately, had been bedridden and confused for several months. When her son and daughter-in-law visited to prepare her for a day of callers and wellwishers, they found her sitting up and looking immaculate. They reminded her that the new minister would be calling on her shortly.

A few moments later came a knock at the door and the doctor arrived for the old lady's weekly examination. The son let him into the house and the doctor showed himself into the bedroom.

After the doctor had examined her, he bade her good-day and left the room to explain to the son that the elderly lady was as well as could be expected. With the doctor gone, the son went in to see his mother and found her mildly upset.

'Fit's wrang, mither?' he inquired.

'He wis affa familiar for a minister,' she sniffed.

TWO WOMEN were in the queue at the Summerhill Post Office and were heard to be discussing their ailments. The larger one had clearly been to the doctor to see about a sore leg, and reported:

'He jist said that if it wis his leg, he widna worry aboot it.

'I jist telt him that if it wis his leg, I widna worry aboot it, eether.'

A RETIRED Garioch vet recalls attending a call to the home of a spinster at Inverurie who was celebrated for her devotion to her two cats. Apparently, one cat had been listless for a long time and was now miaowing and in great pain.

Almost as soon as the vet clapped eyes on the cat, he realised that the animal was heavily pregnant and told the old woman as much.

She was aghast.

'Oh, bit foo could that hiv happened?' she said. 'I dinna let her oot o the hoose, for I'm feart for exactly that kinna thing.'

The vet looked across at a big tomcat filling an armchair on the other side of the living-room.

'What about him?' he suggested.

'Och, nivver,' said the woman. 'That's her brither.'

AN ELDERLY gentleman turned up at a travel agency at Peterhead and seemed reluctant to seek advice, but stood poring over racks of brochures against the wall. Eventually, an assistant went across to see if she could help.

'Aye, lassie, I wis jist winderin if ye dee holidays in Scotland.'

'Yes, we do,' she said. 'Come and take a seat.'

While the old chap seated himself, the assistant gathered

together a pile of brochures and spread them on the counter before him. 'Were you thinking of anywhere in particular?'

'I'd a notion for a wikkend at Dunbar.'

'A very nice place. Would you be going yourself?'

'Na, na, I'd better tak the wife wi me, seein as it's wir ruby anniversary.'

'Oh, a celebration, that's marvellous. Does she know or is it a secret?'

'No, she disna ken yet.'

'Oh, super. She'll get a real surprise.'

'She will that. She's expectin a fortnicht in Tenerife.'

A BLIZZARD was blowing up the Cabrach and the scatter of crofters were becoming increasingly worried about Dod, who stayed by himself and whose but and ben at the heid o the glen was prone to being covered by drifts.

A concerned group gathered and set off to be sure that Dod was all right. They struggled on foot up the glen to where they thought the house would be, but there was no sign. They began probing the drifts with the long sticks they had brought and, eventually, one of them hit the corrugated-iron roof. After a few moments digging, they cleared the lum.

'Are ye a'richt, Dod?' shouted one man down the lum above the raging storm.

'Deein gran,' came a faint voice from inside. 'I'm cosied up and I've plenty o athing.'

'We wis thinkin we'd dig ye oot,' shouted the neighbour. 'It's a hell o a nicht oot here. The sna's blaain lik the verra deevil. We'll be as quick's we can. Can ye wyte or we dig ye oot?'

'Dig me oot?!' came the indignant reply. 'Fit the hell wid I dee oot on a nicht lik this?'

BETWEEN THE wars, Maggie and Tam lived on Deeside and, once a month in the summer, Maggie demanded that

Tam yoke the pony and trap and drive her for the day
to visit her numerous relatives in Buchan. Bored to tears,
Tam passed the days sauntering through the unfamiliar
villages.

'Fit kinna placie wis it that ye visited yestreen?' inquired
one of Tam's friends the following day.

'Nae worth a damn,' said Tam. 'Nae even a decent war
memorial ti read.'

WILLIE LIVED a very spartan life near Keith in a ram-
shackle but and ben at the back of beyond. His dog was
his companion, with two hens that used to lay his breakfast
eggs every morning, but his diet consisted of tins of this and
tins of that.

After one kind lady's Christmas lunch, she packed her
family's leftovers and trudged four miles through the snow
to Willie's cottage. His face was a picture when he saw the
spread being laid before him, but he still gave her a stern
telling off for venturing so far in the snow.

And Willie had a substantial repast, with a paper table-
cloth over the wooden teachest which served as his table,
then Christmas cracker, dram, soup, turkey and trimmings,
trifle, Christmas pudding with brandy and a cup of tea.
She had brought candles, as she knew Willie's old Tilley
lamp was unreliable; bones for the dog and crumbs for
the hens.

After everything had been done to perfection, she decided
she had better get home, as the snow was falling more
heavily. She left, telling Willie that she would return in
a few days to pick up her containers and dishes once the
roads were cleared and the snow melted.

Two weeks later, she ventured back and Willie was
sitting at the fireside, puffing on his pipe. Words were
scarce and she suspected that something was amiss.

'Foo are ye, Wullie?'

'A'right, I suppose.'

She collected all her containers and dishes and, after half

an hour, when still no reference had been made to the meal, she inquired gently: 'Did you enjoy the Christmas dinner I gave you?'

'I did,' he said, 'bit ye'd ower muckle saat in yer gravy.'

GERTIE LOST her teeth after the war and never bothered to replace them. She was happy with her lot and never minded that she was gumsie. Her neighbour, however, was embarrassed about it and invited Gertie over for an afternoon fly cup.

Gertie was a little suspicious, especially since the neighbour was not in the habit of inviting the lower orders in for afternoon tea. However, she knew that the woman's father had not long died, and decided she should at least call to pay her respects to the family.

'Now Gertie,' said the neighbour, sitting her down on the settee, 'I've kent ye a lang time, and I've a proposition for ye.'

'Fit wid that be?'

The neighbour produced a fancy box and pressed it into Gertie's hands. 'Here ye are,' she said, 'as ye ken, ma faither is nae lang deed, and his teeth were barely twa month aul. There wis nae pint beeryin him wi a dear set o teeth, so I jist said til ma man that we'd gie Gertie first refusal.'

ONE DISTRICT nurse wrote to tell us of old Jock, who kept a rusty chuntie (chamberpot) on the sideboard with a beautiful show of lilies growing out of it.

'What a bonnie show o lilies ye hiv, Jock,' she said, and she ventured closer for a sniff, only to discover to her horror that the compost was somewhat pungent, to say the least. In fact, it overcame the scent of the lillies.

'Weel, quine,' said Jock, noticing her distress. 'The secret's a kniv-fae o dung stappit weel doon, bit ye're likely smellin the twa mothballs at the boddim.'

A QUEUE had developed at the chemist's and people

became most alarmed when an ill-natered old-timer got to the front and demanded 'a tube o Semtex'.

The pharmacist suggested that he must have got it wrong. Semtex was a highly unstable explosive much favoured by terrorists. What did he want it for?

'I've a sair-blockit nose and I'm needin it unblockit.'

'Ah,' said the chemist, the mists clearing. 'You mean Sinex.'

A RETIRED farmer was walking through woods near Cults on a Sunday constitutional when a wood pigeon spotted him and covered the lapels of the old chap's brand-new Sunday suit liberally with droppings.

The man's wife, who was strolling with him and who wrote to us, said she had a hard time keeping a straight face when her husband looked disapprovingly at the clartit lapel, then looked up at where the bird was still sitting on the branch of a tree and said simply:

'Min, fit wis the eese o that?'

TWO WOMEN – one as big and bosomy as the other was small and mousy – were standing at an Inverurie bus shelter on a wintry day when slush lay in the gutter and icy winds whipped down West High Street. Our confidant doesn't know how the conversation began, because he joined the queue behind them half-way through, but he jaloused quickly that it concerned a bus running over and killing a small girl's pet dog.

'Of coorse, the bus driver wis affa sorry,' said Bella.

'Affa sorry,' repeated Violet, hanging intently on her companion's tale.

'He couldna stop, ye see. He said there wid hiv been an accident if he'd stoppit. The doggie jist ran oot in front o him. Even the bobby could see that.'

'Even the bobby,' repeated Violet.

'Of coorse, the quinie wis jist brakkin her hert. Brakkin her hert, the quinie. She couldna hiv been mair nor eicht.

And what sorry I felt for her. It wis her doggie, ye see. She wis sobbin. I wis sniffin. Michty, the bus driver wis near greetin, tee. It wis jist tragic.'

'Jist tragic.'

At that, the bus hove in sight. Bella peered at a handful of small change and strode out over the slush and into the roadside. 'Aye, weel,' she said, 'a bonnie little doggie it micht hiv been, bit it's flat as a kipper noo.'

THE WHITE Settler phenomenon – people arriving from outwith the North-east and installing themselves on all sorts of committees within five minutes to run organis- ations in communities about which they know compara- tively nothing – is not new. Many years ago, a Cockney family arrived in Lower Deeside.

One evening, the mother and daughter of the new family decided it would be nice to get to know the neighbours and paid a visit to the neighbouring farm at Newton.

The tenant farmer of the Newton put up with the conversation for some time, but the two visitors were terrible blethers and, anyway, he had great difficulty in understanding the Cockney tongue.

Eventually, impatience got the better of him and he stormed out with: 'Gweed sakes, wummen, will ye haud yer tongues an lat fowk that can spikk, spikk.'

ERNIE, FROM Stonehaven, was proud that he had kept himself in much the same physical condition that he had enjoyed during his Army days, when he had been a physical-training instructor with the Desert Rats. He prided himself on his good health, youthful looks and general trimness.

While on a visit to Aberdeen, he spotted that one of the cinemas had a special deal on for matinee showings, offering cut rates for pensioners. He decided he would take his wife to see a weepie, just as they had in their courting days.

He told the assistant in the ticket booth how old he was and said he would easily show her his bus pass if she needed more proof.

'No, it disna maitter,' said the young girl, 'I can see yer face.'

BILL HENDERSON, an Aberdeen-based financial adviser, told us of visiting a 93-year-old man at Inverurie to go over his investments. The old chap listened carefully as Bill ran through everything in fine detail and eventually pronounced himself happy. Ever the salesman, Bill tried to introduce him to a new five-year bond.

The old boy listened patiently while Bill ran through the sales pitch, then he leaned forward and said quietly: 'I dinna think so, Mr Henderson. At my age, I dinna even buy green bananas.'

. . . and from *Anither Dash o Doric*

GREAT-GRANDMA peered into the week-old bundle of humanity that had been pressed into her bosie. His little hand grasped her crannie and she allowed herself a wee smile. Then she frowned and looked up.

'And fit are ye ca'in him?' she demanded.

'Nathan,' said the proud young mum.

'Awa ye go,' she snapped. 'Ye'll hae ti ca him something.'

OLDER DRIVERS have to take a great deal of criticism for allegedly slow reaction times, which brings us to a tale supplied by a Mr Grant, who lives near Grantown-on-Spey, and was a passenger in a car near Inverurie in 1991 when they had to slow down behind a D-registered saloon being driven by an elderly gentleman.

As they approached a T-junction, where the road widened out into two lanes, the elderly chap switched on his left indicator, so Mr Grant's driver headed for the right-hand lane to turn right. At the same time, the old boy lurched into the right-hand lane, forcing Mr Grant's driver to squeal to an inelegant halt, horn blaring.

The old boy turned right and tootled on, oblivious to the havoc he had caused. Mr Grant's driver decided to tail him to point out his mistake and, a few miles farther on, drew up in front of him and walked back.

'You nearly caused an accident back there,' he stormed. 'Why did you signal left and turn right?'

The old boy, mystified by all the fuss, explained with perfect logic: 'Because ma right flasher's broken.'

LOGIC ALSO featured strongly in the report sent to us from Torphins, of an overheard exchange between two elderly women standing at a bus stop in the village one day in July, 1996. Stagecoach evidently wasn't fulfilling their idea of good service, judging by the tone of their conversation.

'This bus service his jist got worse and worse,' said one to the other. 'There's hardly ony buses and they're aye late.'

'Dinna fash yersel,' soothed the other one. 'It'll sort itsel oot afore lang. If Stewartie Milne keeps biggin as mony hooses as he's deein, a the toons'll seen be oot in the country and we'll hae nae need o buses.'

A PROMINENT landowner and member of the aristocracy whose domain covered large tracts of the North and North-east guarded his privacy zealously, to the extent of enquiring rather brusquely after the business of anyone he found walking on his land.

Early in 1995, he was out for a stroll when he encountered an elderly woman with two small children sauntering up the drive to the big house.

'And what do you think you're doing here, madam?' enquired His Lordship.

'This is ma grandchildren, yer lordship, and I'm takkin

them up til the grass in front o the big hoose for a picnic.'

'Indeed, you are not. You can just turn round and have your picnic somewhere else on ground that belongs to you.'

Her gaze narrowed into one of those determined North-east glowers. 'Ye dinna mind on me, div ye, yer lordship?'

'Should I?'

'Maybe no. Bit mony's the time, fin yer mither wisna aboot, that I gied ye yer bath and changed yer hippens and dichtit yer erse.'

And she sailed on.

SANDY MATHESON was a coach driver in 1973 when he was scheduled to take a party of OAPs from through-out the North-east on a tour to the Italian lakes. He reported standing beside his bus outside the Cowdray Hall, Aberdeen, welcoming his charges as they arrived to begin their off-season adventure.

One of his passengers was a little old lady who had been ferried to the departure point by a little old man, presumably her husband, in a little old Ford Anglia.

'They appeared with enough luggage for half a dozen folk,' wrote Sandy. 'Last of all came a 14-inch port-able TV.'

Sandy stopped them as her husband hobbled up the side of the bus looking for somewhere to stow the TV. 'Excuse me,' said Sandy, 'can I ask fit wye ye're takkin a TV on holiday?'

'I canna miss *Crossroads*,' said the woman.

'Bit they dinna hae *Crossroads* on Italian TV,' said Sandy.

'I ken fine,' she snapped, 'and that's fit wye I'm takkin ma ain TV.'

ELMA MASSIE, now of Aberdeen, tells of two old bodies at a North-east WRI meeting discussing the son of a fellow-member. In the old ladies' opinion, the son was affecting a few airs and graces now that he was a successful businessman in London, and had seemed to forget that he came from good, honest North-east stock.

'Ay,' said one to the other. 'He tries ti spik affa weel-dressed.'

WRITER AND fishing historian Peter Buchan used to tell of leading a party of English tourists round the Fish Market and harbour at Peterhead as a favour to a town councillor.

They seemed to show great interest but, at the end, when Peter asked for questions, one rather clipped lady asked what language it was that people seemed to be speaking to each other.

'That'll be the Doric,' said Peter. 'That's the language we spik up here.'

'It's very strange,' said the woman, looking for a few laughs of approval from her compatriots.

'We manage awa,' said Peter.

'In fact,' said the woman, 'there seem to be an awful lot of strange people up here, full stop.'

'Dinna worry aboot it,' said Peter. 'Maist o them ging awa hame at the end o the summer.'

THE SCENE is Port Elphinstone, near Inverurie, and the Rev. Douglas Lister's Bible class from St Andrew's Church has visited Blythewood Old Folk's Home to attend a service.

Janice Cottier, an Inverurie quine now in exile in the Isle of Man, recalls the weather being baking hot, but the heating in the home being at full blast, for some reason.

'It was uncomfortably hot,' she wrote, 'but this didn't deter a group of ladies from sitting round a blazing fire.'

'I was talking to an old chap who studied the women and then said to me: "See 'at wifies sittin ower there roon the fire. Fin they get ti Hell, they'll nivver ken the difference."'

BACK TO Alford, and another story of Bessie and Maggie. This is the tale which sticks in everyone's mind in the howe. It involves one of the village plumbers, called to the croft to attend a sink blockage or some such.

He picked his way through two dozen glowering cats and clocking hens and had to dismantle part of the cupboard enclosing the sink to gain access to the piping.

As he pulled off the back panel, the faintly ripe odour he had noticed became thick and sickening.

Out flopped a dead cat.

From the look of her, pussy had been there for several months. The plumber crouched, stammygastered, for a few moments, before he reached in, took the cat's remains by the tail and stood up.

Maggie was watching intently. The plumber turned and wordlessly showed her what he had found. She peered up and down at the lifeless form for a few moments, as if unsure what it was, then her face lit up.

'Gweed sakes,' she said. 'I thocht I'd lost that.'

THE WORD 'homogenised' has crept into the vocabulary with mass sales of milk from major companies supplying to superstore, village shop and doorstep.

Without going into the pros and cons of the modern way of processing, we are reminded of the lady who didn't like the change of a milkman in her street.

The ever-so-friendly Fred with a whistle aye on the lips would bring the pinta right up to her door and Mrs McIntosh was disappointed when he retired.

Such are the pressures of modern deliveries that the new milkie would leave the bottles at the old lady's gate, forcing her to make the few yards in her nightie to pick up the milk before she could have her morning cuppa.

Not too pleased on frosty mornings, she challenged the new lad and dared to suggest that she would even give him an extra penny if he would take the milk right up to the door.

'Weel,' said the fastest milkman in the West. 'If at's the wye ye wint it, jist gie's an extra tippence and I'll tak the coo here itsel the morn and skyte the stuff throwe yer letterbox.'

NOW TO a couple who fancied a new car on their retirement. The husband had been used to driving council lorries all his life, with his elevated seat in the cab looking down on the car drivers below.

His wife insisted that they would not buy anything too big. After all, it was just the two of them, and 'a nice wee car'll dee's fine, John'.

The wee Austin was bought and, after a week, John met up with his pals in the local.

'Foo's retirement, John? And foo's the new Austin?'

'Och, retirement's aa richt, I suppose. As for the puddle-louper, it's lik drivin wi castors in yer erse.'

A SIGNALMAN who had worked for most of his career in the confines of a signalbox at Insch was due to retire after forty years' service. A presentation was arranged, much to his disgust, for he 'wintit nae nonsense'.

Handing over a cheque, the stationmaster said: 'Congratulations, Sam. Something of a railway record; forty years in one box.'

Sam's reply, head down with the words muttered from the side of his mouth, was: 'I'll be langer in the neist.'

IAN DAWSON, from Dyce, was known for his straight-faced stories and tells of the time he was in local government and attending council committee meetings.

A colleague was reminiscing on former councillors and asked how old one former acquaintance might be now as he hadn't seen him for ages.

'He's nae interactin wi his environment ony mair,' said Ian.

'Fit?'

'He's deid.'

IT WAS a postie in the Rosemount district of Aberdeen who made us wonder how many tales of the North-east are locked away in the minds of those who are now at the twilight of their lives, with no means of passing on these tales.

The postie in question was dealing with bulk mail, the type that cannot be shoved through the confines of the letterbox, and he told us of delivering the regular book-club new editions of Mills & Boon to an old lady in Rosemount.

In her eighties, and of rural origin, he met her on the doorstep one delivery morning and asked if she still enjoyed reading all these romantic novels.

'Ach,' she said, 'I've been gettin them for years and I dinna wint tae stop noo. The only bits I dinna like are fin they start haulin the claes aff een anither.'

RONNIE WATSON, now retired to Dundee, recalls his Army days in North Africa in 1943. During an eerie lull in proceedings, he was looking round his exhausted comrades, bedraggled, wild-eyed and sore with the heat, when his mate Big Jake from Huntly, said: 'I dinna ken if Rommel's worried aboot this lot, bit they scare the buggery oot o me.'

Mixter Maxter

On the grounds that every decent filing system has to have a Miscellaneous section, we're not going to disappoint anyone. Here are the tales that did not fit easily in one of the other chapters. Look on it as the Lucky Dip you enjoyed so much at the agricultural shows of your childhood.

IN THE mid-1960s, it was not uncommon for small travelling circuses to set up their marquees in showparks even at small North-east villages. On two summer evenings in 1964, the Showpark at Alford was host to one such circus and most of the village young fry and their parents turned out to attend.

At one point came the obligatory spectacle of sawing a woman in half, and the ringmaster announced that the swarthy young man performing the trick had been perfecting his art for more than fifteen years, for it had been his ambition ever since he had been a small boy.

Jimmy Harper, sitting in the audience with two of his four daughters, turned to the man sitting next to him and said: 'That'll be the laddie wi fower half-brithers.'

IT IS said that one elderly member of the aristocracy, whose seat was in Aberdeenshire, had been attending the village show one summer in the 1930s when he had approached the 'Penny A Kiss' stand, behind which stood a pretty young lass of about sixteen. His lordship, who had an eye for the ladies and a wicked sense of humour, approached the stand, fumbled in his waistcoat pocket for sixpence, and presented to the girl, then puckered his wizened lips.

With great presence of mind, the girl turned to an elderly woman in her sixties next to her and said: 'Grandma, maybe you could attend til Lord ——?'

His Lordship opened his eyes and then, quite unruffled, turned to his manservant and said: 'Please attend to this purchase.' And walked off.

ANDREW CRUICKSHANK, the Aberdeen-born actor who went on to play Dr Cameron in the BBC TV version of Doctor Finlay, used to tell a story of attending Aikey Fair as a small boy and being mesmerised by a stall set up by a quack doctor.

The quack was peddling a muddy-brown liquid in small bottles, and hoardings to left and right proclaimed the liquid as a cure for what seemed, to the young Cruickshank, like every ailment and affliction known to man.

'Roll up! Roll up!' shouted the quack 'This miracle liquid will cure every ache, pain and disease known to medical science. It will even cure old age.'

When the crowd began to look sceptical, he announced, with barely a hint of a smile: 'If you don't believe me, I can reveal that I am more than a hundred and twenty years old.'

The crowd's scepticism grew even louder, until one woman looked at the teenage girl taking the cash behind a table stacked with the bottles and demanded: 'Is 'at true?'

'Don't ask me,' said the girl. 'I've only been working with him for sixty-two years.'

AN ESTATE agent was showing a young professional English couple round a country cottage not a stone's throw from the knackery near Kintore. Clearly, the knackery had been busy and, to make matters worse, a nearby farmer was muckspreading.

The couple stood it for twenty minutes until they could stand it no longer. 'Frankly,' said the husband, 'I'm a little surprised you bothered to show us here. Is it always like this?'

'Nae aye,' said the estate agent. Then, realising he had probably lost the sale, added: 'But think on the advantages.'

'What advantages?'

'Ye aye ken fitna wye the win's blawin.'

ONE RETIRED Inverurie woman teacher reports taking a

long-weekend cruise to Shetland with a female friend. The North Sea can be incredibly rough and, on this occasion, lived up to its reputation; barely anyone aboard escaped sickness.

'Don't worry,' said the teacher to her green-faced companion, 'nobody's ever died of a wee bit of seasickness.'

'Oh,' groaned the woman, 'what a peety. It's only the thocht o death that's keepin me alive.'

THE CLERK of works at a North-east town council (who is still alive, so no names) had an office worker who would nip out in the middle of every morning for a swig from a bottle of whisky he kept in the basket of his bike. He would also eat a peppermint to try to hide the smell.

One morning, one of the office-worker's colleagues went out early and swopped the bag of peppermints for a jar of pickled onions. At 10.30, the man duly had his swig of whisky and was aghast to find no peppermints. With no option, he bit into a pickled onion.

A few moments after his return, the clerk of works called him across. 'How long have you worked here?'

'Six years.'

'Exactly. Six years I've put up with whisky and peppermint, but if it's going to be whisky and pickled onion you'll need to find another job.'

IN THE days when Keith was a busy railway junction, one of the platforms was notoriously high and open, and one visitor, accompanied by a Keith woman and being seen away after a holiday, commented on the potential dangers to one of the station staff.

'It's a wonder there isn't a warning sign,' she said.

'There wis a sign,' said the railman. 'Bit naebody at Keith's as stupid as they wid fa aff a platform, so we took it doon.'

A MEMBER of a Central Belt Rotary Club wrote to tell us

about attending a national convention in 1988 and meeting a delegate from the North-east. One evening, they fell to talking about life, love and families and the man from the Central Belt took a picture from his wallet and showed him three boys, pink, scrubbed and smiling.

The man from the North-east took the picture and studied it, smiling. 'That's a nice photie,' he said. 'I wish I hid three loons.'

'Have you not got any family, then?' said the Glasgow man, taking the picture back.

'Aye,' said the North-east man. 'Five quines.'

DEESIDE BETWEEN the wars was known for its Royal connections, but it could claim fame also at the other end of the social spectrum; communities everywhere from Banchory to Braemar were favoured spots for Scotland's tinkers and travelling families each summer.

One tinker was supposedly stopped on the road one evening by a solitary figure, who had obviously been out shooting, and was asked for a match.

Someone who witnessed the incident informed the tinker later that he had had the privilege of being in the presence of the Duke of York.

Shortly afterwards, tinker and 'sportsman' met again. Once again, the sportsman was without a match.

On being asked, the tinker once again produced a match but, as he handed it over, remarked: 'It's a terrible thing that a man lik me is supposed ti keep the king's bairn in spunks.'

THE SCENE is a roup (auction sale) at a craftie at Rora. Sandy Bell is auctioneer and George Mackie is showing the goods. 'Right,' says Sandy, as George holds up a double-burner glass lamp, three-quarters full of paraffin, 'fit for this lump, noo?'

There is some mildly animated conversation, but no concrete interest.

'Come on, noo,' says Sandy, 'there's aboot a gallon o paraffin in't.'

'Aye,' shouts Willie Duncan from the floor, 'and aboot a fortnicht o wikk.'

SANDY WAS forever fa'in doon throwe his English. One evening, while about to start compering the local-hall concert, he announced:

'We're affa sorry, bit Mrs Soutar canna be wi's the nicht ti play the pianna. She's decomposed. Hooivver, Mrs Mack, the doctor's wife, his agreed ti be the prostitute and, as abody here kens, she'll dee a gran job o't.'

FORMER PAGE Three girl Linda Lusardi was invited one year to open the Oldmeldrum Sports, a considerably brave departure from the normal roll of celebrities invited to do duty.

'Fa's this openin the show?' one worthy was heard to ask his companion.

'That's that deem that taks aff her claes in the papers,' said the other.

The two of them studied the ample Miss Lusardi for a few moments as she walked round the ring, then the first turned to the second:

'A gey change fae Maitland Mackie, onywye.'

A TAXI firm in the glens of West Aberdeenshire was asked for a good, safe driver for a wedding, and he had to be a teetotaller so that the bride's parents could be sure that their daughter's day wouldn't be spoiled.

'Canna help ye there,' said the boss. 'We hinna onybody lik that, bit I can gie ye a driver that ye'll nivver fill fu.'

THE REASON Aberdonians like golf, Edwin Reid informs us, is that the better they get the less wear there is on the clubs.

THE SCENE is Briggies, the local name for the Allargue

Arms at Cockbridge, and mine host Airchie is sweelin the glasses waiting for the men of the Lonach Pipe Band to return from their outing to the Nethybridge Games. The last of the tourists have bedded down and suddenly, on the stroke of midnight, the Lonach Men explode on the place to tell of the success or otherwise of the piping competition across the hills.

As if to prove the exercise, out come the pipes, drums, busbys and all and soon the bar is filled with music and marching – a dirl enough to wake the dead.

It certainly stirs one couple whose bedroom is right above the action. They uptail and slink off into the night without so much as a goodbye.

Three weeks later, one of the pipers asked Airchie: 'A'thing a'richt, Airchie?'

'Michty aye,' said Airchie. 'A couple walkit oot athoot peyin on the nicht o the Nethybrig Games, bit I got the best o them; he left his pyjamas ahin, and I've been weerin them ivver since.'

THE LONACH is celebrated as one of the most historic community events in Scotland, drawing an audience from around the world. Its traditions are many and various, but the most notable is the march of the Men of Lonach, when one hundred and thirty kilted hielanders tramp seven miles of Strathdon, stopping off along the route to partake of drams provided by hosts of castle and ha'.

Dr Innes, a son of the schoolhouse, was actually domiciled in Humberside, but dutifully travelled north on the appropriate August Saturday to be sure that tradition was upheld.

'Tell me, Dr Innes,' one of his Yorkshire colleagues asked him one year, 'what is it that takes you north at the end of August every year?'

'Ah, my freen,' he said. 'It is my most pleasant duty to dispense one hundred and thirty drams to the Men of Lonach on their march.

'And then I spend the rest of the day trying to avoid one hundred and thirty thirsty highlanders determined to stand their hand back to me.'

NOT OFTEN is the Lonach spoiled by bad weather, but when the heavens do open stories abound of previous experiences in the rain. Willie Gray, the bard o Briggies, regaled those within earshot as to how rain seldom stopped work on farms. He took his fellow-clansmen back to the days when steam-driven threshing engines powered the threshing mills on visits to farms at the tail end of the hairst.

'Aye,' said Willie, 'I mind ae eer fin the hivvens open't and the rain nivver deval't. We stoppit in the efterneen for wir fly-cup and nivver got yokit again.'

'Oh?' said an attentive clansman next to him. 'Wis it ower coorse ti yoke?'

'Na,' said Willie. 'Ma cup widna teem.'

WHEN YOUR co-author (the one that presents radio programmes) visited the Edinburgh studios of BBC Radio Scotland to record a dance-music programme, he went into the reception area to ask if he could use the phone to contact home.

Mission accomplished, the receptionist asked him: 'Tell me, are there words that cannot be translated from the English into the Gaelic?'

'Oh, aye,' he said. 'Wirds lik television, ile rigs, helicopters and the like, I wid imagine.' Then he thought for a moment. 'By the by, fit wye are ye askin me? I dinna hae the Gaelic.'

'Oh,' said the receptionist, 'so what was that you were speaking on the phone to your wife?'

And they say the Doric is not a language.

THE DAYS of the travelling dramatic societies in the North-east are sadly over. The favourite plays were in the Doric, of course, and included such as Mains Wooin and The Wee Reid Lums.

Abbie Moir had been a leading light with his Culter group over many years and recalled a visit to the Powis School Theatre in Aberdeen, where they were staging The Red Barn Mystery. Abbie, as William, had gently persuaded Maria out to the barn. The sound and lighting effects denoted a terrible night of thunder and lightning, and heightened the suspense, as the audience was aware that William had murder in mind.

The villain was down on his knees with his hands round Maria's neck. Abbie's acting must have been powerful and compelling, indeed, for one lad up in the balcony, for he jumped up, unable to contain his temper any longer, and shouted:

'Let er go, ye bugger! Ye're chokin er!'

UNTIL THE early 1980s, Aberdeen cars had the registration letters RS and RG, while Aberdeenshire had AV and SA. Naturally, the registration autorities had to be careful of any offensive combinations of letters, which was why the registration LAV was never issued. They also decreed that ARS should never be issued, which shows presumably that the diktat came from Down South.

They were certainly quite unaware of the local pronunciation, because they permitted (and still do) ERS.

ALL NORTH-EAST villages are fuelled on gossip. In many cases, what is not known is made up or embellished into a decent scandal out of all proportion to the truth. There are many stories, but the most succinct came from a native of Rhynie, describing her village.

Both of us would like to stress to Rhynie residents that we have nothing against Rhynie, and that this came from one of your own.

'If ye fart at the tap eyn o Rhynie, it's intil a heap o dirt by the time it's oot at the fit.'

A MEMBER of the check-in staff at Aberdeen Airport was said to have been treated to disciplinary action after he hung a piece of mistletoe over the check-in desk. When departing passengers asked what the mistletoe was there for, he would tell them: 'So you can kiss your luggage goodbye.'

BILL WAS a fiddler who owed more to enthusiasm than expertise, but still he persisted in entertaining at concert parties. In the early 1960s, he established himself down the bill in a short variety season at the Tivoli Theatre, Aberdeen, largely by diversifying into comedy, at which he was considerably better than the fiddle-playing.

One evening, he arrived later than usual for his call, and a new stage-door hand stopped him, pointed at the violin case and asked what was inside.

Bill was indignant. 'It's a machine-gun,' he said.

'Thank hivven for that,' said the young lad. 'I wis feart it wis yer fiddle.'

JIM LAWRIE was a doyen of Aberdeen hotel porters in the early 1970s, and did duty at several city hotels, but the famous story about Jim concerns the time he showed an important American gent up to his room.

The American was one of the most awkward customers Jim had encountered, putting him to all sorts of needless trouble, changing his mind about the order in which his cases had to be brought up, and so on. To cap it all, he didn't even offer a tip.

Half an hour later, the American called down to reception and asked for the bellboy to be sent up. Jim duly appeared at the door.

'Say, maybe you could come in and show me where the air-conditioning controls are,' drawled the Yank.

'There's nae air-conditionin in this hotel, sir,' said Jim drily.

'No air-conditioning?' gasped the Yank. 'Ya hear that,

honey, there ain't no air-conditioning in this hotel. Tell me, boy, what am I supposed to do if it gets too hot or too cold?'

'Weel,' sighed Jim. 'I suggest ye open a windae or fart.'

. . . and from *Anither Dash o Doric*

A BANFFSHIRE man who prefers not to be named told of his grandfather, who had recovered from a serious illness in the late 1950s and, having had one scare, thought he would like to make some arrangements for the future, so he went to the undertaker and explained he would like a coffin to keep in his shed, just so he could be sure that he would be laid away properly when his time came.

'We cwid mak ye een,' said the undertaker. 'Finest Oregon pine, polished brass plates, satin linins, silk tossles, fifty-one poun, the lot.'

'Michty, I wis doon at the jiner the ither day and he said he wid mak me a boxie for twinty poun.'

'Weel, g'awa til the jiner if ye please, bit I'll gie ye a fortnicht and yer erse'll be oot the dowp o't.'

IN THE early 1930s, an aunt of Helen Mills, now of Spey Bay, was maid to a Mrs Thompson at Braes of Enzie farm, near Buckie. One spring Sunday, on her day off, the maid picked an armful of catkins while walking by the River Spey, intending to use them as an arrangement she was doing for a special occasion for her mistress at the farm.

On her way home, she met Lily and Lizzie, two local quines also out for a walk.

'Oh, what bonnie pussy-willas,' said Lizzie. 'Fit are they for?'

'They're for a do at Mrs Thompson's,' said the maid.

As the two girls walked past, the maid heard Lily turn to Lizzie and mutter: 'I nivver kent doos ate catkins.'

THE LADIES of one North-east golf club had signed up for a weekend outing to Spey Bay. For an extremely reasonable fee, they were entitled to return coach travel, a round of golf on the Saturday, an evening meal, entertainment, a night's accommodation, a hearty Scottish breakfast, another round of golf and lunch before heading home.

When Kath discovered that the entertainment was to be a popular band known as The Seagulls, she was delighted and could hardly wait for Saturday evening.

Fortified by a good meal and a sherry or two, Kath was sitting in the lounge tapping her feet and beaming at the musicians. She was apparently unaware that The Seagulls had had to call off at the last minute and had been replaced at short notice by another combo entirely.

This would not normally have caused any problem but, with the effect of the sherries, Kath decided to visit the loo between numbers. Walking past the band that she still imagined was The Seagulls, she grinned mischievously at the lead singer and inquired:

'Hiv ye poopit on onybody lately?'

BILL PIRIE was leading a group of novice hillwalkers along a particularly remote and tricky part of Glencoe when they were confronted with a ledge narrow enough to cause some of the participants a little concern.

Bill assured them that every precaution had been taken and that, as long as they didn't do anything silly, it was as safe as crossing the road.

'But just suppose een o's dis slip,' said one middle-aged woman. 'Fit should we dee?'

'Weel,' said Bill, 'the best thing wid be snappin yer heid as hard as ye can til the left.'

'Fit dis that dee, like?' asked the woman.

'It disna stop ye fa'in,' said Bill, 'bit what a rare view ye get on the wye doon.'

WHEN THE film *Fatal Attraction* was released, queues

built up outside the cinema in Aberdeen. One evening, Frances Robb was sitting engrossed in the story with two or three of her chums from work.

In the scene where Michael Douglas and Glenn Close were overcome with passion in the kitchen and began rolling from worktop to table to floor and back again, Frances said she became aware of the middle-aged couple in the row in front.

The woman leaned to the man and said: 'You nivver get workit up lik him.'

And the man leaned back and said: 'He gets peyed for't.'

IT'S SAD to see the decline in boatbuilding round our coast and the demise of the wooden-built hulls requiring special skills handed down through the generations.

It was the annual holiday at Turra and, with the usual closedown of all market-town activity, Jock and Aggie would 'hae a day oot' in the Austin 7 and headed for Buckie.

Once they had parked the motor, they would have a daunder round the harbour and stopped by Herd and Mackenzie's Yard, where work was in full swing.

The foreman took them in and was explaining one particular art as the caulker was hard at work. It was pointed out that the process, with the tradesman deftly hammering in the waterproof material, was to pack the seams between the planks of the bottom of the boat to prevent leakage.

Jock came up with the sensible suggestion:

'Wid it nae be easier pittin the boords closer thegither?'

A SLIP of the tongue from your co-author who is also a Highland Games commentator.

It was at Oldmeldrum Sports in June and a competitor made his debut having travelled all the way from the Isle of Arran to compete in the heavy events.

On introducing the young athlete as he threw the light hammer, over the Tannoy came:

'That was young Scott Clark throwing the hammer aa the wye fae the Isle of Arran.'

To which judge Bob Aitken retorted: 'Michty, Robbie, at's fairly a new record for Meldrum.'

WE WERE reminded of a tale going back to the days of the whaling by Bob Smith's excellent book *Buchan – Land of Plenty*.

There has always been great rivalry between the fishing ports of Fraserburgh and Peterhead. In the days of the whaling, Peterhead was making a name for itself with something like thirty whalers in the Arctic, well ahead of the tally from Fraserburgh.

Not to be outdone, a notice appeared at the Broch Harbour, proclaiming

HALF OF OUR WHALING FLEET SAILED YESTERDAY
THE OTHER HALF WILL LEAVE TOMORROW

What it didn't say was that half of the fleet was one ship; there were only two whalers sailing from the port.

SEVERAL years ago, when Aberdeen were playing an Italian side in a European football tournament, the usual exodus of supporters had driven, bussed and flown to Italy to roar on the Dons.

After the match, one forlorn supporter had been celebrating (or, more likely, drowning his sorrows) and had become detached from his party and had missed his flight.

In a haze of alcohol, he realised that the best course of action was to thumb a lift north to Turin where he might be able to convert his ticket for a later plane.

And so, still much the worse for wear, he came to be standing at the side of a rain-spattered autostrada, sticking out his thumb and hoping that someone would stop in time.

Eventually, a coach pulled in and our man, soaking jacket up around his ears, peered up at the driver as the door hissed open. Unknown to him, the coach was full of Dons supporters beginning their own long journey home.

'Eh, per favore,' said our man in halting Italian. 'Torino?'

'Sorry,' said the driver. 'Wid Bucksburn be ony eese?'

ON A VISIT in 1996 to Dingwall to record a programme for Radio Scotland's *Take the Floor* your presenter of that medium sought refuge after rehearsal in a wee pub in the centre of the town.

He was surprised to find only three people at the bar counter; a couple of Gaelic teuchters and a gentleman the waur o the weer who spoke with a real North-east tongue.

Ordering a refreshing lager, Robbie must have given away by his tongue that he was of the North-east and this was richt inta the barra of the gentleman, who turned out to be a retired farmer from the Howe o Cromar.

After regaling the wee company with a lecture on the Doric, in the Doric, his two pals started conversing in Gaelic to wind him up.

'Ach,' snapped Mr Douneside, 'pey nae attention; I've tellt them afore the Doric's jist as important as their yab-yab-yabble in the Gaelic.'

Then he turned on his two companions. 'Listen til es, you twa. If it wisna for fowk lik me, and fowk lik him,' – pointing to Robbie, whom he didn't recognise – 'and if it wisna for Robbie Shepherd, the Doric wid be deid.'

OVERHEARD AT Lawrence of Kemnay, an enthusiastic salesman was dealing with a chary client.

'And I suppose,' said the customer, 'that ye'll tell me, lik ivry ither car salesman, that it's jist hid ae careful owner?'

'Ay,' said the salesman, adding with admirable honesty, 'and a half-dizzen ither haimmerin buggers.'

THE LATE John Stammers, for long Registrar of Births,

Deaths and Marriages at Braemar, often told this story against himself.

The wife of one of the village hotel managers, not native of Deeside, had given birth to a daughter, and the father approached John about registering the birth.

Our Braemar registrar asked what the child's name was to be and was told: 'Tamara.'

A bit nonplussed, John replied: 'Och aye, Tamara will dee fine. Fit time?'

JAMES SLATER, a Buckie fisherman, aye maintained that he had managed to get English classified as a foreign language when he did his National Service in the Royal Engineers.

At his interview on joining the Army, he was asked if he spoke any foreign tongue.

He replied: 'Ay, English.'

'What is your native tongue?' he was asked.

'Doric. It's spoken in North-east Scotland.'

He was lectured and told that regional accents were not separate languages, but James was thrawn and challenged the corporal.

They agreed that if he said something in Doric and the corporal did not understand what he said, the NCO would have English entered as a foreign language on his record and get the pay supplement for having an extra language.

Put to the test, James launched immediately into: 'Gin I hiv till eese a graip tae shuffle sharn an dubs for mony a wikk, I'll ca ee the feelest gype wi a gey clarty doup at ivver I clappit een on.'

He got his pay supplement.

IT APPEARS that all Observer Corps stations round the Granite City were on a party line connected with Centre and everybody listened in. Centre reminded all observers that they must report every aircraft. So it was that this conversation drew many a chuckle from those on duty.

'Newtonhull here. Spitfire, bearing 270, height sax fit, gyan north, over.'

'Centre here. Are you sure? Over.'

'Newtonhull replyin. Aye, over.'

'Centre here. Check co-ordinates again in two minutes, over.'

'Newtonhull here. Spitfire bearing 271. Height sax fit, proceeding north, over.'

'Centre here. He's impossibly slow. Check again, over.'

'Newtonhull here. He's nae that slow; jist on the back o a larry, oot.'

WE GO BACK to the days of few cars and fewer tourists. The usual gathering of locals had assembled in the middle of Cornhill when a fancy open-topped motor car screeched to a halt and the occupant beckoned the town worthy Frankie to come hither.

Neither Frankie nor anyone else moved. Further beckoning had no effect and the toff shouted in an irritated voice: 'Are you deaf, man? Does this road go to Portsoy?'

'Na,' said Frankie, hands in pockets, 'it bides here.'

A MEMBER of the Lonach Pipe Band recalled taking exception to a Strathdon laird who had been heard to say in a speech at some function that 'Life has been made very much more difficult in recent weeks by those pipe bands.'

Who knows what war might have broken out if someone else had not worked out that what the laird had actually said was:

'Life has been made very much more difficult in recent weeks by hosepipe bans.'

THE WHOLE village of Dunecht used to turn out for the travelling cinema shows in the village hall. The blinds would shut and the whirr of the projector would send a sense of great expectation round the assembly.

Aggie was a weel-kent and weel-liked craiter, but she was just a wee bit backward intellectually. She had seldom been anywhere out of the village and fair enjoyed the weekly treat at the makeshift cinema.

They happened to be showing *Old Mother Riley* one particular week and Aggie's guffaws of laughter soon had every head in the hall turning.

During one particular scene, where Ma Riley went straight through a strae-rick on her motorbike, Aggie, overcome by the drama of it all, jumped to her feet and ran back up the hall howling: 'Goadalmichty!'

THE FOLLOWING week, it was a Roy Rogers picture. The hero had just been shot and, to all intents and purposes, appeared dead. Having checked to make sure he was dead, the villain was about to leave the saloon when Roy rallied and started to rise.

Aggie, so mightily relieved to see that he was alive after all, and petrified in case the baddie would look back, skirled: 'Lie doon, Roy, ye feel bugger!'

IT HAS been rumoured, but never confirmed, that the recording mannie of the two of us had his car broken into recently.

His radio was gone, as were tapes of the Beatles and Oasis, his son's favourites, and his wife's easy-listening cassettes. Left behind were cassettes of himself belting out his bothy ballads.

The police are still looking for someone with an ear for music.

A FRASERBURGH skipper took his crew to a harbourside hostelry at the end of a successful trip because he wanted to stand his hand. On asking everyone what they would like, he found that each one replied: 'A pint wid dee fine.'

All except Tommy, who was reputed, literally, to have a very big mouth.

'Weel, Tom, and fit aboot you?'

'Ach, skipper, I'll jist hae a moofae.'

'Damn the linth, ye'll tak a pint lik abody else.'

The Ones That Got Away

We're certainly not suggesting that the people who sent us these tales were passing them off as the genuine article when they owe more to myth and fancy, but let's say both of us had heard variations on these themes over the years and we didn't want to risk the truth of the rest of the book by including them among the others. Still, some of them were too good to waste so, with a warning that you enter this chapter at your own risk, feel free.

KEEPING A nationally-renowned pipe band going is a costly business and needs a good deal of investment and fundraising. The story goes that the Oldmeldrum and District Pipe Band decided on a door-to-door collection, and each band member was dispatched to one particular part of town.

One came to a neatly kept pensioner's house and knocked on the door. An old body came and asked what he wanted.

'I'm collectin for the Oldmeldrum and District Pipe Band,' he said.

She cupped her hand to her ear. 'I'm a bittie deif,' she said. 'Ye maun spik up.'

'I'm collectin for the Oldmeldrum and District Pipe Band,' he said a little more loudly.

She screwed up her face in puzzlement. 'Na,' she said. 'Canna mak ye oot ata. Fit is it ye're sikkin?'

'*I'm collectin for the Oldmeldrum and District Pipe Band!*' he shouted.

She shook her head again and, realising he was working against impossible odds, he shook his head, gave her a weary wave and turned and walked back down the path. He clattered the gate shut behind him.

'Watch ma gate!' she shouted angrily.

'Ach, bugger yer gate,' he said.

'Aye,' she said. 'And bugger yer Oldmeldrum and District Pipe Band.'

THE MOTHER of a kitchie-deem at a big country house in Formartine marched up to the door and demanded to see the laird.

'It's oor Nellie,' she said. 'We think she's pregnant wi a yer capers and we'd like ti ken fit ye intend deein aboot it.'

The laird looked flummoxed for a moment then said: 'All right. All right. If she really is pregnant, I'll give her ten thousand pounds and put another twenty thousand in trust for the baby. Will that keep it quiet?'

The woman had the wind taken from her sails, but recovered enough composure to say: 'Fairly that. And if she's nae pregnant, will ye gie her anither chunce?'

AN ABOYNE man went in for his morning paper, whistling. The newsagent was struck by how cheery the customer was, and said so. 'Aye,' agreed the man. 'It's ma birthday the day.'

'Well, congratulations,' said the newsagent. 'How old are you?'

'Foo aul d'ye think I am?'

'Fifty?'

'Na, I'm jist forty.'

The man went along to the baker, for his morning butteries, still whistling.

'Ye're real happy the day,' said the baker.

'Ma birthday,' explained the man.

'Congratulations,' said the baker. 'Foo aul are ye?'

'Foo aul d'ye think I am?'

'Fifty?'

'Na, I'm jist forty.'

The man went along to the grocer, for his pint of milk, still whistling.

'Ye're real happy the day,' said the grocer.

'Ma birthday,' explained the man.

'Congratulations,' said the grocer. 'Foo aul are ye?'

'Foo aul d'ye think I am?'

'Fifty?'

'Na, I'm jist forty.'

The man went out to the bus stop, still whistling and stood behind a woman in her eighties, waiting for the bus to Ballater.

'Michty,' she said. 'Somebody's affa cheery the day.'

'Ma birthday,' explained the man.

'Congratulations,' said the old woman. 'Foo aul are ye?'

'Foo aul d'ye think I am?'

She studied him up and down. 'Well,' she said warily, 'I widna like ti say, bit I ken a foolproof wye that I can tell.'

'And fit's that?'

'If I gie ye a richt slubbery kiss and then rub yer backside.'

The man was a little taken aback, but looked at the little old lady and thought there was no harm in it, so he bent forward to receive a wet slubbery kiss and then stuck out his behind so she could give it a good stroke.

'Now,' he said. 'Foo aul am I?'

'Ye're forty.'

He was amazed. 'Foo on earth did ye ken that?'

'I wis stannin ahen ye in the queue at the baker's.'

WE WON'T trouble you with the famous-but-hoary old 'Aa ae oo?' story, but we liked the tale of the country loon visiting the Lecht ski slope for the first time, struggling to put on his skis and looking up plaintively to ask:

'Fit fit fits fit fit?'

THEY SAY that a farmer visited the Smithfield Show for the first time late in his career and was amazed by the sights and sounds of the Big Smoke. He decided to stay on for an extra day just to savour London life.

All was going well until his braces snapped, perhaps with the exertions of climbing up and down the steps into the Underground. He nipped into a post office just off Regent Street.

'I'll tak a pair o yer galluses, ma dear,' he informed the woman behind the glass once he got to the head of the queue.

'I beg your pardon?'

'A pair o galluses, ma dear. I'll tak a pair o galluses.'

'Galluses?'

'Galluses. Ye ken. Braces. For haudin up yer brikks.'

'Braces? I'm sorry, sir. This is a post office.'

'I ken that fine.'

'But we don't sell braces in a post office.'

'Well, they div at Auchnagatt.'

A YOUNG mother from Fraserburgh was becoming increasingly fed up with her brood's incessant demands for sweeties. On one shopping trip to Aberdeen, her patience finally snapped. 'Lord,' she shouted. 'If ye dinna stop aetin a that gulshach, ye'll be that fat that folk'll aye be lookin at ye.'

On their way home on the bus, the boy noticed a very pretty, but heavily pregnant, young woman getting on, and he began smiling to himself. Not many miles along the road, she caught his gaze and he smiled at her. She smiled back and his smile broadened into a grin and a steady stare.

Eventually, she became puzzled and leaned across to him. 'Div I ken you, or div you ken me?'

'I dinna ken ye,' said the boy, 'bit I ken fit ye've been deein.'

A MACDUFF skipper put to sea and after a few hours decided to grab a bit of sleep and instructed the youngest and greenest member of the crew to keep watch and report if he spotted anything that he thought the skipper should know about.

The lad scanned the horizon intently and eventually, just

after the skipper had nodded off, burst in on him and said: 'Skipper! Skipper! There's a seagull!'

'For ony sake, laddie!' stormed the skipper. 'Ye wakken me up ti tell me that! I telt ye that ye should only disturb me if it wis something that wid interest me! And ye wakken me for a bliddy seagull!'

'Oh, bit I think ye'll be interestit in this seagull, skipper. It's sittin on a rock.'

TWO FARMERS boarded the train at Torphins and were sitting smoking their pipes in silence when a commercial traveller entered.

'Good morning, gentlemen,' he said brightly. He was met with glares and silence.

The traveller left the carriage at Banchory and bade the farmers farewell with: 'Good day, Gentlemen. A very pleasant day to you both.'

One farmer looked at the other, took the pipe from his mouth and said: 'A gabbin vratch.'

THE MAN from Littlewoods called to tell the Donside farmworker that he had won almost £1 million on the pools. The man was shocked and delighted all at once, and invited the Littlewoods representative inside, apologising for the state of the house, but his wife was away visiting her parents for a few days.

They went through the paperwork, then the Littlewoods man asked him how he thought he'd spend the money.

'Oh,' said the farmworker, 'This his a happened real sudden. I hinna hid time ti think. I suppose I'll likely hae a holiday. A new car. Maybe I'll buy masel a new hoose. See ma relations in Australia. A cruise, maybe.'

'And what about your wife?' said the Littlewoods man. 'What will she be buying herself?'

'Lord,' said the farmworker, 'dinna tell me she's won the pools, as weel.'

ANOTHER POOLS winner – this time a Buchan farmer

– was asked how he would spend his windfall. Would he buy a fancy car? A villa in Portugal? Go on a world cruise? Or just retire?

'Na, na,' he said. 'I'll jist fairm awa til the money gings deen.'

WHAT'S THE difference between stubborn and that good Doric word thrawn? The dictionary will tell you that there is no difference; that thrawn is merely another word for stubborn (a N. Brit. Dial. word, to be precise).

But there's a big difference between stubborn and thrawn, as the following apocryphal story shows. An illness had threatened to disrupt the activities of a Formartine primary school. Two boys had very sore tummies, which the school nurse put down to constipation. Both were sent home with wee notes of the ailment and the suggested remedy.

Mother No. 1 read the note and went for a bottle of syrup of figs from the chemist. 'Noo, Johnnie,' she said. 'The nursie says ye maun tak yer syrup o figs for yer constipation.'

'I will not.'

'Ye will sut.'

'Winna.'

And so the battle commenced with no suitable outcome. That's stubborn.

Over at Mother No. 2's: 'Noo, Billy, the nursie says ye maun tak yer syrup o figs for yer constipation.'

'I will not.'

'Ye will sut.'

'Winna.'

And so a ding-dong battle ensued, much as before, except that in this case, Billy was worn down eventually by sheer fatigue and, to get the matter over and done with, relented slightly.

'OK,' he said. 'I'll tak the syrup o figs.'

His mother duly administered it.

With a furious scowl on his face, half born of rage and half of the dreadful taste of the medicine, Billy stormed off, saying: 'A'richt. I've taen it noo. I've taen the bliddy syrup o figs.

'Bit I winna poop.'

And that's thrawn.

THERE IS nothing more enjoyable than a country wedding reception in a village hall. North-east folk seem to be more at home there than at a posh hotel, yet the food, the decoration and the formal proceedings are the same.

At a wedding a few years back up Deeside, the main guests were seated at the top table, including the minister beside the bride's mother and the bride's father seated next to the groom's mother, and so on, and so on. The usual set-oot.

Along came a waiter with the drinks and he asked the bride's father if he would care for a whisky.

'Michty aye. Fairly, fairly,' said the father, and a dram was duly set down in front of him.

The waiter moved along the top table and, coming to the minister, asked if he, too, would like a dram.

'Do you not see I'm a man of the cloth?' said the minister. 'And you offer me whisky? How disgusting. How inappropriate. I would rather commit adultery.'

At which the bride's father handed back his glass, saying: 'Michty, I didna ken we'd a choice.'

THE YEAR that Aberdeen's seagull population exploded was certainly 1995, when glorious weather brought a most unwelcome problem to The Toon – fouling, scavenging and din throughout the city. The letters columns in the newspapers were full of debate for weeks.

Two lads of simple mind were having a walk around the Harbour when a seagull spotted one of them well and truly, and scored a direct hit, all over the lad's head and shoulders.

'God dammit,' he said. 'Look at me noo. Hiv ye bit paper, Sandy?'

'That winna dee ony good,' said Sandy. 'The damnt bird's miles awa or noo.'

TWO SONS of New Deer, who had left for work in London and had retired there, had been unable to make it home for the funeral of one of their former cronies who had died, but they turned up together the following summer, by which time the headstone was in place, but it had subsided badly and was leaning at a jaunty angle.

Davie found a piece of wire at the gravedigger's bothy and managed a makeshift repair by tying the wire securely to the headstone and tying the other end to a nearby fencepost. He intended going round to see the widow and explaining that maybe someone had better try a more permanent repair.

The two of them were just about to leave the cemetery, when two of the village's older ladies walked past the stone and stopped to look.

'Wid ye credit that?' said one to the other. 'Geordie dee't nae sax month syne, and he's got the phone in already.'

GIBBY AND Erchie had gone on a package holiday to Rome with their wives. One evening, while the girls went sightseeing, the lads repaired to a bar and asked the barman for a sample of the local brew.

'What about this?' said the barman, showing them a bottle of creme de menthe. 'This is what the Pope drinks.'

'If it's gweed enough for His Popeness, it's gweed enough for us,' said Gibby. 'Gies twa pints o yer creme de menthe.'

The barman obliged and watched them, amused, as they struggled through the creme de menthe and were soon near unconscious. The next thing they knew, it was six in the morning and they were streaked out on the floor of a bus shelter in a Rome suburb, both with splitting headaches, dry mouths and shaking limbs.

'Michty,' said Gibby, trying in vain to haul himself upright. 'If that's fit the Pope drinks it's nae muckle winner he gets aff planes and fa's on his knees.'

A WIDOW was being comforted on the night before the funeral by her daughter and two of her closest neighbours. One of the neighbours remarked that the widow seemed to be remarkably composed, and hoped that the grief wouldn't hit when all the friends and family had departed and suddenly she realised she was on her own.

'No,' said the widow, looking at her husband in his coffin. 'I'll be fine. Geordie spent a wir mairriet life oot drinkin and bowlin and gamblin and playin aboot wi ither weemin. This is the first nicht in years I've kent far he is.'

MYSIE AND Dod from Strathbogie had been trying for almost ten years to start a family when, one day, Mysie decided she had better go for a pregnancy test. Later, the doctor studied the results, then leaned across the consulting desk and patted her hand.

'Well, Mysie,' he said, 'I'm delighted to tell you that after all these years, you're expecting.'

Mysie was overcome, almost on the point of tears with relief and happiness. 'Oh, doctor,' she said, her voice quavering, 'that's the best news we could hiv hopit for. I winder if I could hae a shottie o yer phone so I could phone Dod at his work.'

The doctor smiled and pushed the phone towards her. She dialled the number, waited a few moments and asked to be put through to Dod at his desk.

'Oh, Dod, Dod,' she said. 'I've got news for ye. I'm pregnant!'

There was a deep silence at the other end, followed by a cautious: 'Fa's spikkin?'

BERTIE WAS one of those townspeople before the war

who were celebrated for their slow wit, but who were never really as slow as townsfolk liked to think. Bertie's stance was on the Plainstones at Banff, where he would lean and watch the world go by, and most of the townspeople would give him a cheery wave as they went about their business.

It was a favourite sport of the more exalted townsfolk from the southern end of town to go for a Sunday stroll, see Bertie in his usual spot on the Plainstones, and go up to try a little test to amuse their wives. A man would hold out a shilling in one hand and a threepenny bit in the other and tell Bertie he could have his pick to keep.

Bertie always chose the 3d.

When a nearby shopkeeper could bear the insult to Bert no longer, she bustled out of her shop the following morning and said: 'Bertie, surely ye ken that the nobs are jist takkin ye for a feel. I saw them yestreen, jist like I've seen them ilky Sunday. They offer ye a shillin and a thripny and they think it's great fun fin ye jist tak the thripny. Fit wye div ye nae tak the shillin? It's worth four times as muckle.'

'I ken that, mistress,' said Bertie. 'I ken that fine. Bit if I took the shillin, they widna come back the next Sunday.'

CHARLIE AND Mary were out for a Sunday runnie in their new Austin one day when a police patrol car pulled out of a hiding place at the end of a farm road and began following them. Sure enough, a few miles later the blue lights went on and Charlie drew into the side.

The bobby strolled up and tapped on the window, and Charlie rolled it down.

'Fit's yer hurry?' said the bobby. 'This is a forty-mile-an-oor area. Ye were deein at least sixty.'

'I wis jist deein forty,' said Charlie firmly.

'Oh, bit I'm sorry sir, ye were deein sixty, onywye.'

'Forty,' repeated Charlie.

'And I'm tellin ye sixty.'

Mary leaned across. 'Oh, for ony sake, officer, dinna argy wi him fin he's been drinkin.'

IN 1974, just before the last local-government reorganisation, households in places where boundary changes were likely were sent explanations from the Scottish Office as to what was being proposed, how it would affect them and also inviting representations.

At one out-of-the-way farm in the Cabrach, the son of the house took the letter to his elderly mother and read it out to her. She listened closely, without saying anything. When he had finished, she thought deeply for a few minutes.

'So fit dis it bile doon til?' she asked.

'Well,' said the son, 'fae fit I understand, we winna be in Banffshire efter next year, we'll be in Moray District.'

'I see,' mused his mother.

'Bit it says here that if we wint ti complain, we should write til this address.'

'I see.'

'So will we complain?'

'No, no, we'll jist leave it. I couldna thole anither Banffshire winter.'

ELSIE WAS happily married to Bert and they had five children. Then Bert died. Shortly, Elsie married Dod, and they had four children. Then Dod died. Before long, Elsie married Chae and they had five children. Then Chae died. Not long after, Elsie died.

At her funeral, friends filed past the casket, and one lady murmured: 'See foo nice Elsie looks in her goon, and isn't it nice they they're together again?'

The woman behind her asked: 'Fa div ye mean? Elsie and Bert?'

'No,' said the woman.

'Well, ye mean Elsie and Dod?'

'No.'

'Elsie and Chae?'

'No,' said the lady. 'I mean her knees.'

WHEN AN Aberdeen woman gave birth to triplets, the story was reported in the *Press and Journal*, and a medical expert interviewed explained that it was still a rare occurrence and happened probably only once in 20,000 times.

'Michty,' said one reader to another. 'I'm amazed she'd ony time for her hoosework.'

AT ONE Aberdeen Airport open day, a flying club from down south was offering pleasure flights in a World War I biplane and was doing a roaring trade, despite the fact that, as the day wore on, the wind was getting stronger and stronger.

Last in the queue were a farmer from New Pitsligo and his wife. By the time their shottie came round, the wind was really quite strong. 'It's up to you,' said the pilot. 'Air Traffic Control says we're OK for the moment, but I have to warn you that it will be quite bumpy. You won't be frightened?'

'Michty, nivver a fleg,' said the farmer. 'I'm a fairmer fae Pitsliga wi a big overdraft at the bunk. There's nae nithing can scare the likes o me. Dee yer warst. Bit if it's gaun ti be really bumpy, we'd be due a special price, I'm thinkin.'

The pilot said he would cut his usual price of £30 to £10. Then, to add a little piquancy to the proceedings, said that the special price would apply only if the farmer was able not to scream or shout throughout the whole of the flight. The farmer accepted the challenge readily.

Not wanting to lose the £20 difference, the pilot put the plane through the worst of the windy weather, and then tried a few aerobatics, with spirals, rolls and loop-the-loops.

But the farmer said nary a word throughout it all.

When they taxied back to their part of the airport apron, the pilot helped the farmer out and accepted the £10 note that was offered.

'Well,' said the pilot. 'I must say I admire your cool. I certainly wouldn't have expected you to be able to stay quiet through all of that.'

'Weel,' said the farmer, 'I will admit I near said something fin the wife fell oot.'

IN THE days when the sleeper service south was used far more than it is now, it was a regular occurrence for the sleeping-car attendants to be asked to rouse passengers in time to get off at a particular stop.

One October evening, a sales rep boarded the train at the Joint Station, Aberdeen, and went immediately to find the attendant to impress upon him the importance of being in Berwick the following morning and told him that no matter how fast asleep he was the attendant was to kick him off the train, if necessary.

In the morning, the sales rep awoke to find himself in King's Cross, London. He went to find the attendant and the language he used was bluer than a Rangers shirt.

When his fury finally died and he stamped off, the attendant's supervisor came round and asked what all that had been about. 'I've never heard language from a passenger like that in all my career,' he said.

'That's nithing,' said the attendant. 'Ye should hiv heard the mannie I threw aff at Berwick.'

FINALLY, THERE's no truth in the rumour that when Robbie Shepherd found an old bottle of cough mixture in the bathroom cabinet, he sent his son, Gordon, out in his pyjamas to play in the sna.

. . . and from *Anither Dash o Doric*

A MAN visited his GP complaining of a severe rash across his back which seemed to be spreading and was maddeningly itchy. The GP examined him and was aghast at what he found. 'You're suffering from a severe form of jungle contagion,' he told his patient.

'Is that serious like, doctor?'

'Well, it tends to spread very quickly – twenty-four hours is about the limit of it – and three-quarters of cases result in a painful, agonising death.'

The patient swallowed hard. 'Michty, doctor, is there nae cure?'

The doctor thought for a moment. 'G'awa ben the corridor,' he said, 'and lock yersel intil that wee roomie at the eyn. We'll pit ye on a special diet o Ryvita and Kraft cheese slices.'

'And will that cure me?'

'No, bit it's a we can slide aneth the door.'

AN AMERICAN woman on holiday in Aberdeen was being driven round the city when the car had to stop at a pelican crossing. The crossing began its usual peeping.

'Say, what's that noise?' she inquired of her host.

'Oh, that's the noise so that blind people know when the crossing's active.'

'Gee,' said the American woman, 'in the States, we don't let blind people drive cars.'

AN ELDERLY North-east couple owned a holiday cottage which they let out during summers. One summer, the husband discovered that the family who had rented it were nudists and had been cavorting in privacy behind the hedges in their birthday suits.

The old man was alarmed that the neighbours might

find out, or even call the police, so he rushed home to tell his wife.

'Ye'll nivver guess, Jeannie,' he said, breathless. 'Fit div ye think they're using the craftie for?'

She shook her head.

'A nudist bare-nakit setoot. Not a stitch. Oh, Jeannie, fit'll we dee?'

Jeannie thought for a moment. 'There's jist ae thing we can dee,' she said.

'Fit's that?'

'Double their rent.'

THE WOMAN who owned the village craft shop went storming into the butcher to complain that the lamb chops she had bought the previous Saturday had shrunk so much in the pan that they were hardly worth the bother of cooking and serving.

'Well, if we're hearin complaints,' said the butcher, 'ye're as weel kennin that yon jersey I bocht fae ye for ma wife's birthday shrunk sae muckle in the wash that it widna even fit ma dother's dollie noo.'

'Weel,' said another customer, who had been listening intently, 'I doot the chops and the oo come aff the same lambie.'

BERTIE REID was a steady smoker and his wife had had no luck in trying to get him to stop, so she tried shaming him into quitting.

'Bertie,' she said, 'Alfie Duncan doon the road, he's stoppit smokin. Foo's that for willpower, eh? That's a rale man, if ye ask me. Stoppit smokin jist lik that. Willpower.'

Alfie stood up. 'I'll show ye willpower,' he said, and for the next seven weeks he slept alone in the spare room.

Mrs Reid took it in good part at first, but she missed Bertie at night. Finally, one night she tiptoed to the spare room, opened the door slightly and whispered:

'Bertie? Are ye sleepin, Bertie? Alfie Duncan's startit smokin again.'

AN ELDERLY woman crofter not a million miles from Foggieloan won the WRI monthly competition for redcurrant jelly and was given a choice of prize. She could have had a felt hat made by a fellow-member, or she could have had a straw hat made by the same woman.

'I'll tak the straa hat,' said the winner after hardly any deliberation at all.

'Fit wye did ye tak the straa hattie?' enquired the hatmaker later. 'The felt hat cost twice the price and took near double the time ti pit thegiether.'

'Aweel,' said the elderly winner, 'the felt hattie wis bonnie, richt eneuch, bit the straa hattie's better for me. Fin it's ca'ed deen, I can feed it til the nowt.'

THANKS TO the Kennethmont reader who sent us this story. We're not sure that this is tasteful enough for the book, so those of a nervous disposition should turn the page.

She claims that while she was a nurse at Inverurie Hospital, not long after it had become an exclusively geriatric unit, she had been accompanying a doctor who was attending a sad old craiter who had just been admitted and whose prognosis was not good.

'Tell me,' said the doctor kindly, 'have you ever been bedridden before?'

'Oh, aye,' said the old lady. 'Mony a time. And twice in the back o a cairt.'

ECHT SHOW was wearing to a close and Sandy had spent just a little too long in the beer tent with his cronies. Out in the fresh air, the warm whisky was taking its toll and he started making his weary way home on foot.

The road and the ditches seemed to merge and he stumbled off the side of the road up to his waist in water.

Striding out of that as best he could, he continued his journey and was relieved to find a telephone box on his road home to Midmar.

Dialling his wife, he said: 'Sorry, quine. It's been a fairish day. I've jist faan intil a ditch. Can ye come for me?'

'Bit far are ye ringin fae?'

'Fae the erse doon.'

THERE WERE not that many phone calls to the household of Jock and Sadie in their cottage by the farm on the road ben the seashore by the Broch – at least not when Jock was at home.

He would often have business with his float to uptail and ca the nowt from some particular mart, which meant an early start.

So it was that the phone rang one morning with Jock, for once, enjoying the extra snooze before rising time.

Jock hirpled, pyjama trousers nearly tripping him up, to the phone downstairs.

Upstairs, Sadie could hear Jock's muffled: 'Hello? Hello?', followed by an expletive or two.

Sleepy-eyed Jock crept back up the stair to be greeted with an anxious: 'Fa wis 'at?'

'Ach,' he said. 'A wrang number. Some fisher billie, I doot, for he wis speirin gin the coast wis clear.'

EVERY NEW Year, the telephone lines become red hot as far-off and near-at-hand relations get into sentimental mood. A Guid New Year is sung again and again, and promptly forgotten in the subsequent sober moments of the day.

Tam was not one of those revellers. He liked his bawbees too much to spend on such ploys. However, the phone did ring at four one New Year's morning and it was Tam who was kicked out of bed to answer the call.

His anxious wife – thinking, at that time of the morning,

that a close relative might have passed away – prodded Tam as he crept back into bed.

'Fa wis't? Aathing aa richt?'

Tam grunted.

'Some damnt gype sayin it wis a lang distance fae Australia. Ony feel kens at. I jist clappit doon the phone on him.'

A FARMER from Auchnagatt was instructed by his wife to nip in past Duncan Fraser's when he was in town and get her a new bra for a forthcoming farmers' ball.

On arriving at the requisite counter, he was asked which size?

'Oh lassie, I dinna ken muckle aboot sic things.'

'But you know the size of your wife, surely. Any idea at all?'

He scratched his head for a minute or two, then ventured: 'Size thirteen.'

'Thirteen?' said the assistant. 'Surely not. How do you arrive at that?'

'Weel,' he said, 'my bonnet's sax and sivven-eichths and it haps jist een o them.'

AN UNIDENTIFIED Deeside woman told us of a Mrs Brown from a village up Deeside. Mrs Brown is supposedly a traditionalist and bemoans the demise of more and more of the local grocers' shops. Her own village shop is still on the go, but changes must be made to keep up with the big stores.

On entering the shop recently, she asked for her usual 'steen o tatties'.

'Sorry,' said Alex from behind the counter. 'We dinna sell that ony mair. It's kilos noo.'

'Ach weel,' she said, 'jist gie's a steen o kilos.'

IT SEEMS that most infant and nursery teachers keep spare

clothes in case of accidents at school with all the excitement of the early days of lessons.

One wee girl at a Fraserburgh primary unfortunately had such an accident and wet her pants. The teacher dutifully changed the wee lass and sent the wet pair home in a plastic carrier bag.

You can imagine the commotion in the bus the next day when wee Lee-Anne, sitting with her father, spotted the teacher at the front.

In a loud voice, the wee lass said:

'Miss MacGregor, my dad's got your knickers in his pooch.'

THREE YOUNG lads from around the Cruden Bay area were in a huddle one day discussing their respective fathers and venturing as to which dad would be the bravest.

'My faither's affa brave,' said Tam. 'He saw twa robbers comin oot o the Clydesdale Bunk at Peterheid and he rugby-tackelt them baith, haudin them doon till the bobbies arrived. Aye, my dad's the bravest.'

'Na, na,' said John. 'My dad heard o somebody that hid faan doon the cliffs o the Bullers o Buchan. Athoot a safety harness or onything, he gaed doon the brae face and bade there directin the helicopters. My dad's the bravest.'

But Willie was silent.

'Fit aboot you, Willie?' they asked.

'Na,' said Willie sadly. 'My faither's a cooard.'

'Fit wye?'

'Ilky time ma mither's awa seein ma unty in Edinburgh for the wikkend, he needs the wifie in fae next door tae sleep wi him.'

EVEN AS late as the 1960s, neighbouring farmers round the Garioch used to take it in turns to host entertainments for their friends.

Hilly came into the kitchen where his wife was preparing the goodies for the forthcoming party. She was looking somewhat doon in the moo, and hubby asked what was wrong.

'Ach,' said Jean. 'It's this trifle. I hinna ony o yon silver ballies that Bogie's wife hid on her een last year.'

'Nivver fash,' said the loving husband. 'I'll jist teem a car-tridge ower the heid o't and naebody'll be ony the wiser.'

The night of the party came and went and, next morning, Hilly was calling in past his neighbours to see how things were doing.

'Weel, Mains, hid ye a gweed time last nicht?'

Ay, man, it wis a grand affair. Jist ae thing. The wife wis haulin on her draaers this mornin and she shot the cat.'

Glossary

A gentleman's guide to Doric as she is spak

Acquant	Familiar
Aenoo	Just now
Aeten/aetin	Eaten/Eating
Affrontit, black	Ashamed, embarrassed
Aneth	Beneath, below
Athoot	Without
Auler	Older
Aye-aye, min	Hullo there, good fellow
Bannocks	Large, thin pancakes
Barrafaes	Barrowloads
Bathert	Bothered
Beets	Boots
Ben	Through
Bide	Stay
Birstled	Burned, sizzled
Blaad	Damage, spoil
Bocht	Bought
Boddim	Bottom
Bosie	Embrace, hug, cuddle
Brakk	Break
Bree	Liquid residue
Breein	Straining water from
Bugfae	Bagful
Ca nowt	Transport cattle

Caafies	Calves
Ca'ed deen	Worn out
Cairt	Cart
Claes	Clothes
Claik/claikin	Gossip/gossiping
Clappit	Clapped, patted
Clart	Slap on to excess (v.)
Clart	Farmyard manure, slurry (n.)
Clarty	Dirty
Climmed	Climbed
Contermacious	Awkward, deliberately difficult
Coo'ard	Coward
Coorse	Bad, coarse
Coup	Tip, topple, empty out
Craiters	Creatures
Crochlie	Infirm, unsure of step
Cubbidge	Cabbage
Cuttie	Pipe
Cwidna	Could not
Damn the linth	(mild expletive)
Deemie	Young woman
Dicht	Wipe
Dipper	Tank for sheep-dipping
Dirlin	Rattling, ringing
Dizzen	Dozen
Dockens	Dock leaves, a tenacious weed
Dominie	Headmaster (usu. male)

Doon aboot/in the mou	Depressed, out of sorts
Dother	Daughter
Dowp, Doup	Backside, posterior (anat.)
Drookit	Drenched
Dubs	Mud
Dungars	Overalls, dungarees
Dyeucks	Ducks
Ee	You
Eese	Use
Eest tae	Used to
Efterhin	Afterwards
Eneuch	Enough
Eyn	End
Faan, faun	Fallen
Far	Where
Fash	Bother, upset
Feart	Afraid
Feel	Stupid
Ficher	Fiddle, fumble, interfere (v.)
File	While
Fit's Adee?	What's wrong?
Fit wye	Why
Flechy	Infested with parasites
Fleg	Fright
Folly	Follow
Foo	How
Footer	Fiddle, nuisance, waste of time

Forrit	Forward
Fusslin	Whistling
Futret	Weasel or stoat (not a ferret). Now usu. derog.
Gad sakes!	Yeuch! (exclam.)
Gadgie	Chap, fellow
Ganzie	Sweater, cardigan
Gaur	Make
Gey	Quite, really
Grieve	Farmworker's foreman
Gulshach	Sweets
Gype	Idiot, poltroon (usu. male)
Hairst	Harvest
Hale	Whole
Haps	Covers
Haud gyan	Keep going
Haulin	Pulling
Hich	High
Hinder end	End (taut.) pron. 'hinner'
Hirply/hirpled	Hobbly, unsteady/hobbled
Hoo'er	Prostitute (or unpleasant (adj.))
Ilka/Ilky	Each/every
Ill-natered	Not of sunny disposition (usu. married female)
Ingin	Onion
Interficherin	Interfering with
Intimmers	Insides (anat.)
Ivnoo	Now, at this moment

Jaloose	To reckon or fathom
Jinkin	Ducking and diving, chicaning
Jints	Joints (anat.)
Keekin	Looking impishly
Kirn-up	Mess
Kittle up	Enliven, invigorate
Kniv-fae	Fistful
Larry	Lorry
Lees	Lies
Linth	Length
Loon	Boy
Losh be here!	My goodness! (exclam.)
Loup/louper	Jump/jumper
Louse	Loose
Lowsin time	End of day's work
Mairriet	Wed, married, betrothed
Mischanter	Mishap
Mochey	Grey, drab, dreary
Moofae	Mouthful
Nae wye	Nowhere
Neen	None
Neep	Turnip
Neist	Next
Neuk	Corner
News	Chat, discussion (n.)
Nickum	Imp, mischief-maker
Nivver fash	Don't worry

Nowt	Cattle
Oo	Wool
Oots and ins	Kirby grips, hairpins
Orraloon	Young farm labourer
Orraman	Farm labourer
Ower the heid	A surfeit, in excess
Pints	Laces
Pish	Urinate
Ploo	Plough
Plooky	Pock-marked, enjoying a surfeit of pimples
Plottin	Sweating
Pooch	Pocket
Poodin	Best part of any meal
Priggin wi	Pleading with
Puckle	A few
Pucklie	Small amount of
Pyokie	Small bag containing something
Quaet	Quiet, peaceful
Quine	Girl
Raivelt	Confused
Rale	Real
Raxin	Stretching
Reid hett	Red hot
Rickle	Pile, haphazard collection
Riggit	Ready (usu. sartorial)
Rikkin	Smoking, steaming
Rive	Rip, tear or wrench

Roch grun	Rough ground
Rodden	Rowan
Roost	Rust
Rooze	To anger, inflame
Rowin	Transporting (also wrapping)
Saat	Salt
Sair	Sore, painful
Sair grun	Barren land
Sair-made	Troubled, in pain
Satty	Salty
Scuddlin	Idling, lazing (usu. while sartorially challenged)
Scutter	Delay
Semmit & draa'ers	Vest and pants
Sharn	Slurry (usu. agricultural)
Sheen	Shoes
Shooed	Sewed, sewn
Sikkin	Needing, requiring
Siller	Money, cash
Skelpit	Smacked
Skirlie	North-east delicacy, best with onions slightly burned
Skite/skyte	Slide
Skitter	Diarrhoea
Slubber	To slurp (onom.)
Snod	In good order
Sook	Suck
Sookit-lookin	Puckered, wrinkled (usu. corpses or accountants)

Soon	Sound
Soss	Mess
Sotter	Mess
Souter	Shoemaker
Spad	Spade
Speir/speirin	Ask/asking
Spew	Vomit
Spile	Spoil, damage
Spunks	Matches, lucifers
Stairvin	Freezing
Stammick	Stomach
Stammygaster	Astonishment
Stappit	Rammed, jammed, forced
Steen	Stone
Steen caul	Stone cold
Straa	Straw
Stots	Bounces
Strae-ricks	Straw stacks
Stravaigin	Wandering, exploring
Styter	Stumble, stagger
Sup	Small amount (usu. liquid)
Swack	Supple, fit
Sweir	Reluctant (adj.)
Sweir	Swear (v.)
Taakin	Engaging
Teem	Empty
Tekkie	Outing, trip, visit

Tidee	Commotion
Tirred	Undressed
Toonsers	Indigenes of Aberdeen (derog.)
Trachled	Troubled, worn out, exhausted
Trock	Rubbish, debris, garbage (usu. concrete n., not abstract)
Trump/trumpin	Tramp, step/tramping
Twa pun	Two pounds (weight)
Tyauve	Struggle (pron. 'chaav')
Vratch	wretch
Waur nor	Worse than
Waur o the weer	Worse for wear
Weerin	Wearing
Wheen	Good few
Wheepit	Whipped
Widin	Wading
Win	Get
Wrang spy	Mistaken identity
Wug	Wave
Wye	Way
Wyte	Fault
Wytin	Waiting
Wyve	Weave
Yestreen	Previous evening
Yokie	Itchy
Yokin	Starting work

Where Credit's Due

AS WE said in the Foreword, we can't claim all the glory for the tales you have read here. This book wouldn't be as full and varied as it is without the help of the many people who took the time and trouble to write down their favourite family stories, professional stories, schoolday stories and chance eavesdropping stories and sent them to us. We are exceptionally grateful, and the least we can do is record their contribution. If we have missed anyone out, we're sorry.

Thanks to Esma Shepherd, Alison Harper, Jack from Kincorth, Les Wheeler, Frances Patterson, Peter Nicol, Andy Duff, Norman Connell, Jack Kellas, Mrs M. Robertson, Peggy Veitch, Sandy Mackie, Margaret Ross, Major Rory Haugh, Joyce Everill, James Stewart, A. Gill, Ian Middleton from Arradoul, Alistair Ross, Hamish Mair, Johnnie Duncan, T. Munro Forsyth, Geordie Stott, V.B. Taylor, R.P. Nicol, A.J. Harper, Norman Harper sen., Isabel Ford, Bill McCormick, Nancy Forsyth, Ogilvie Thomson, Bryan Smith, Chris Clark, Gordon Argo, Ron Anderson, Eric Stevenson, Bill Duguid, Ethel Simpson, Mary Kennedy, Margaret Black, Nan Sandison, G.E. Smart, Douglas Mutch, Lilianne Grant Rich, Ray McIntosh, Edwin Reid, Mary Campbell, Carolyn Smith, Rena Gaiter, Mrs L. Christie, Ron Knox, Alec Cameron, Gordon Milne, Eileen McHardy, Miss B.H. Ritchie, P. Dawson, Willie J. Taylor, P.J. Duncan, Helen Walker, Graham MacLennan, Chrissie Sutherland, Chrissabel Reid, John Stewart, Frances Jaffray, Sandy Watt, Lorna Alexander, Sybil Copeland, Aileen Jason, Sandy Mustard, Evelyn Leslie, John Duff, Douglas Schaske, Christine Birnie, Ethel Baird, Doug Hampton, the Rev. Jim Scott, Jimmie Mitchell, Charles Barron, Mabel Mutch, James Morrison, Duncan Downie, Leslie and Hilda Innes, Kenny Mackie, Donald Manson, Joan Christie, Bill Mathers, Graham Maclennan, Mrs M. Riddoch, Bob Knowles, Andrew Foster, Bill Connon, H. Walker,

Isobel and Peter Slater, Douglas Merson, Norah Hardy, Violet Thomson, Yvonne Cormack, Jess Robertson, Donald McAllister, Jim Glennie, J.O. McHardy, Elizabeth Hendry, Willie Smith, Bill Mowat, Elma Massie, Ian Dawson, Ronnie Watson, Helen Mills, Bill Pirie, Frances Robb, Janice Cottier, Nicholas and Cameron Harper, Jim McColl, Mary Gerrie, Eric Wilson, Karen Buchan, Nanny and Hilda, Joe Watson, John Dear, George Durward, David Ross, Eileen Dunn, Sheila Innes, Jimmy Lees, Dr Pat Macdonald, Jimmy Irvine, Bill Shand, Kathie Ross, the Rev. Gordon Smith, the Rev. Charles Birnie, Margaret Mathison, Sandy Matheson and dozens of others who wrote and requested anonymity, as well as thousands who, over the years, have entertained us with their conversation.

Robbie Shepherd and Norman Harper
Aberdeen, 2003

And Finally

A third, all-new volume is at the planning stage. If you know of a classic example of North-east humour – true stories only, please – do write to us. If you seek anonymity, it's guaranteed, but we don't want your stories to go to waste.

Drop us a line at: Dash o Doric, Birlinn Ltd,
10 Newington Road, Edinburgh EH9 1QS